Diving & Snorkeling

# Monterey Peninsula
## & Northern California

Steve Rosenberg

LONELY PLANET PUBLICATIONS
Melbourne • Oakland • London • Paris

Diving & Snorkeling Monterey Peninsula
& Northern California
- A Lonely Planet Pisces Book

3rd Edition – June, 2000
2nd Edition – 1992, Gulf Publishing Company
1st Edition – 1987, PBC International, Inc.

Published by
**Lonely Planet Publications**
192 Burwood Road, Hawthorn, Victoria 3122, Australia

**Other offices**
150 Linden Street, Oakland, California 94607, USA
10a Spring Place, London NW5 3BH, UK
1 rue du Dahomey, 75011 Paris, France

**Photographs**
by Steve Rosenberg (unless otherwise noted)

**Front cover photograph**
Diver in Diablo Pinnacles kelp forest

**Back cover photographs**
Octopus with eggs in abalone shell
Sea lion cavorting at the Monterey breakwater
Kelp bed off the Big Sur coast

The images in this guide are available for licensing
from **Lonely Planet Images**
email: lpi@lonelyplanet.com.au

ISBN 0 86442 775 1

text & maps © Lonely Planet 2000
photographs © photographers as indicated 2000
illustration © Lonely Planet 2000
dive site maps are Transverse Mercator projection

LONELY PLANET and the Lonely Planet logo are
trademarks of Lonely Planet Publications Pty Ltd.

Printed by H&Y Printing Ltd., Hong Kong

# Contents

# Diving in Northern California   35

# Monterey Bay Dive Sites   44

# Carmel Bay Dive Sites   67

# Marine Life 114

# Diving Conservation & Awareness 119

# Listings 124

# Index 132

# Author

## Steve Rosenberg

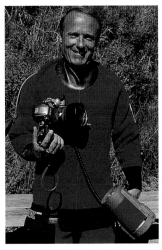

MICHAEL MCKAY

Steve has been a professional underwater photographer and photojournalist since 1980, when he began writing articles on travel, photography and nature for various U.S. publications. He is a member of the Society of American Travel Writers and has now published several books and hundreds of articles. He has also won more than 250 awards for his photography in national and international competitions. Thousands of his images have appeared in books, magazines, posters, stamps and as artwork worldwide. He lives in Northern California and has explored the waters off Monterey and the north coast for more than 30 years. Steve also practices law in Alameda, California, and has been involved in diver access litigation, successfully preserving diver access at various locales in the Monterey area.

## From the Author

I'd like to thank my many friends and dive buddies for their support, encouragement and constant abuse in the course of diving sites and gathering information for this and prior editions of the guide. In particular, I would like to thank my special buddy, Darlene Tarantino; my longtime buddy and co-conspirator, Al Huelga; Laurie Huelga; my daughter and newest dive buddy, Shannon Rosenberg; and a lengthy cast of confederates including Rob Walsh, Ben Tetzner, Susan Crawford, Carl Miller, Roger Hess, Rhonda Cooper, Art Hazeltine and Kathleen Shannon; Marg and Matt Hill of Dive Crazy; Charlie Lorenz of North Coast Discoveries; Dan Gottshall of Sea Challengers Books; and Roslyn Bullas, Sarah Hubbard and Debra Miller of Lonely Planet Publications.

## Photography Notes

Steve's preferred photographic equipment includes Nikonos RS-AF cameras and lenses, Nikon SB-104 and Sea & Sea strobes, with Ultralite arms and accessories. Most of the images in this book were shot on Fujichrome Velvia film for close-ups and Fujichrome Provia, Fujichrome Astia and Kodak Ektachrome E100SW for wide-angle photographs.

## Contributing Photographers

Most of the photographs in this book were taken by Steve Rosenberg. Thanks also to Reggie Brown, Ken Howard, Michael McKay and Shannon Rosenberg.

## From the Publisher

This third edition was published in Lonely Planet's U.S. office under the guidance of Roslyn Bullas, the "Divemaster" of Pisces Books. From the coral-encrusted Fish Tank, Sarah Hubbard edited the text and photos with invaluable contibutions from Wendy Smith, Debra Miller and Rachel Bernstein. Emily Douglas designed the cover and book. Navigating nautical charts were cartographers Patrick Bock and Sara Nelson, who created the maps, and Alex Guilbert, who supervised map production. Hayden Foell illustrated the Steinbeck sidebar. Lindsay Brown reviewed the Marine Life sections for scientific accuracy. Portions of the text were adapted from Lonely Planet's *California & Nevada*.

## Lonely Planet Pisces Books

Lonely Planet acquired the Pisces line of diving and snorkeling books in 1997. The series is being developed and substantially revamped over the next few years. We welcome your comments and suggestions.

## Pisces Pre-Dive Safety Guidelines

Before embarking on a scuba diving, skin diving or snorkeling trip, carefully consider the following to help ensure a safe and enjoyable experience:

- Possess a current diving certification card from a recognized scuba diving instructional agency (if scuba diving)
- Be sure you are healthy and feel comfortable diving
- Obtain reliable information about physical and environmental conditions at the dive site (e.g., from a reputable local dive operation)
- Be aware of local laws, regulations and etiquette about marine life and environment
- Dive at sites within your experience level; if possible, engage the services of a competent, professionally trained dive instructor or divemaster

Underwater conditions vary significantly from one region, or even site, to another. Seasonal changes can significantly alter site and dive conditions. These differences influence the way divers dress for a dive and what diving techniques they use.

There are special requirements for diving in any area, regardless of location. Before your dive, ask about environmental characteristics that can affect your diving and how trained local divers deal with these considerations.

---

## Warning & Request

Things change—dive site conditions, regulations, topside information. Nothing stays the same for long. Your feedback on this book will be used to help update and improve the next edition. Excerpts from your correspondence may appear in *Planet Talk*, our quarterly newsletter, or *Comet*, our monthly email newsletter. Please let us know if you do not want your letter published or your name acknowledged.

Correspondence can be addressed to:
**Lonely Planet Publications**
**Pisces Books**
150 Linden Street
Oakland, CA 94607
email: pisces@lonelyplanet.com

# Introduction

Diving in Monterey Bay and Northern California isn't for everyone. Divers who jump into these chilly, nutrient-rich waters must have a hankering for excitement, a desire to witness awesome tapestries of shapes and colors, and a yen to experience the unusual. Majestic rock formations, playful marine mammals, vast underwater kelp forests, and a kaleidoscopic array of colorful invertebrates and other marine animals inhabit the waters of inshore reefs and offshore pinnacles. Diving on days when the visibility is more than 50ft (15m) and the sun bursts through the cloak of fog or clouds is like floating through a giant redwood forest—an awesome and addictive experience. On days when the plankton explodes and visibility decreases, the water takes on emerald hues and a close inspection of the reef surfaces reveals new wonderment. In this miniature fairyland, resplendent nudibranchs, ornate plume worms and feathery barnacles are interspersed with flowing fields of diminutive strawberry anemones.

Diving in Northern and Central California is quite different from warm-water diving. Cold water temperatures require that you wear at least a quarter-inch (7mm) wetsuit or a drysuit. The emphasis on beach diving, coupled with the

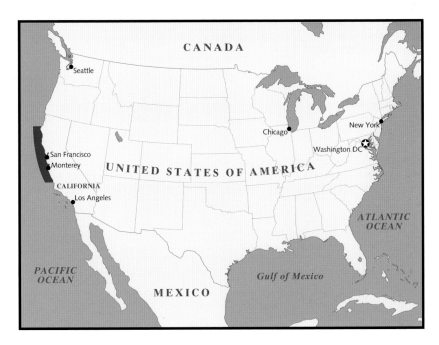

often-rough conditions, requires training that isn't needed to dive in most other parts of the world. If you're a novice diver or if you're new to California diving, it's a good idea to buddy up with an experienced local diver. Consult the experts at local dive stores; they can give you up-to-date information on charter boats as well as current weather and water conditions. Some stores and local instructors or divemasters also offer guided tours to some of the more popular sites.

If you are new to California diving and choose to dive without the benefit of a local diver's experience, don't overestimate your ability. Choose a site that is well protected from the open ocean. Do not attempt to beach dive in an area where there is heavy surf or strong currents, and keep in mind that tides and wave action can drastically change dive conditions very quickly. This is especially true on the north coast, where many sites are exposed to the prevailing winds and swells that roll in from the northwest. Even experienced divers contact a local dive store for information on diving conditions before setting out for a dive site and, on a moment's notice, will cancel their plans if the conditions aren't right for a safe, enjoyable dive excursion.

This guide is a useful tool for resident as well as visiting divers, regardless of skill level. You'll find detailed information about the best and most popular dive sites within Central and Northern California's five major dive regions— Monterey Bay, Carmel Bay, the Big Sur coast, the Sonoma coast and the Mendocino coast.

The information given for each dive site will help you dive safely and get the maximum enjoyment from each dive. Each dive site description includes the location, dive entry and exit points, range of depths, on-shore facilities, and a brief description of the underwater topography and marine life. This information should help you select the dive sites that are most appropriate to your skill level and personal interests.

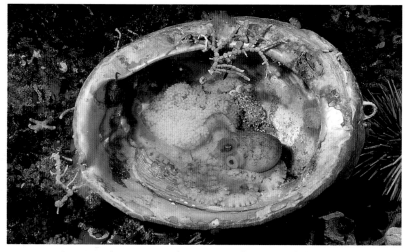

An octopus lays its eggs in the protection of an empty abalone shell.

# Overview

The Central and Northern California coast is well known for its rugged shoreline. Rocky headlands and promontories rise vertically from the sea, alternating with stretches of recessed shore bordered by sand and gravel beaches. Though rugged, the coast is quite straight, broken only by the Monterey and San Francisco Bays. North of San Francisco, there are a number of smaller bays along the San Andreas fault line, which follows the coast and extends into the sea just south of Cape Mendocino.

## Geology

About 18,000 years ago, vast portions of North America were covered by immense sheets of ice. The formation of these ice sheets lowered the sea level by more than 400ft (120m), exposing previously submerged coastal areas. South of the ice sheet, new coastal plains emerged and, in California, extended as much as 60 miles (97km) beyond today's shoreline. Rivers formed and cut channels through the plains, creating deltas and estuaries along the new coast. (These beds cut into the surrounding rock are now submarine canyons, such as those that reach into Monterey and Carmel Bays.)

When the ice melted about 12,000 years ago, the sea level rose again, flooding low valleys and river mouths. Water flooding seaward from the melting inland glaciers swelled the rivers, causing erosion that produced some of California's most striking coastal cliffs and wide beaches; the soft rock formations (sandstone, clay and shale) eroded, while the harder rock developed into headlands. The result was the formation of massive cliffs, which jut into the water and alternate with recessed stretches

SHANNON ROSENBERG

Cliffs line much of the California coast.

**11**

of sandy beach, giving the coast a scalloped appearance. The continental shelf slopes gradually from the shore down to approximately 600ft (185m) before plunging sharply into the depths of the Pacific Ocean. In the coastal areas above the shelf, marine life feasts on a plentiful supply of nutrients, fostering a riotous profusion of both vertebrate and invertebrate life.

## Shaping the Shores: Currents, Waves & Tides

The currents and the strong winds of the Pacific team up to generate some of the most powerful waves in the northern hemisphere. The waves and currents gnaw at the shoreline, continuously sculpting the beaches and wearing down the rocky headlands. These waves and currents also help bring nutrients into shallow areas near shore, as do upwellings, which pull cold, nutrient-rich water up from the depths to help nourish life in the coastal zone.

The southward-flowing California Current is part of the Pacific Ocean current system. Spawned by winds and the rotation of the earth, warm equatorial waters off the coast of South America flow west to Asia, then head north in the vast Kuroshio Current. The Kuroshio Current passes Japan and turns east, heading for North America. Along the way, it picks up cooler water drawn down from the Arctic and eventually turns south, becoming the California Current, which parallels the Pacific coast until it reaches the equator, where it heads west. As it sweeps along the coast, the current carries billions of microscopic plankton and other marine plants and animals that feed the coastal marine life.

Tides also have a critical effect on California coastal formation. There are usually two high tides and two low tides daily along the Pacific coast. The movement of tidal waters near the shore causes tidal currents. As the tide rises, the waters flow toward shore causing a flood tide. During ebb tide, the water moves out, exposing low-lying coastal areas. In many places, these tides play a critical role in transporting sediment.

Wave action is a primary factor in coastal formation.

# Geography

The cities along California's central and northern coasts are as diverse as the shoreline itself. The San Francisco Bay Area is the jumping-off point for the central coast to the south, as well as the northern coastal towns. It is a melting pot of cultures and lifestyles whose influence reaches far and wide. Outside the Bay Area, there are no large population centers in this region of California, though there are a few notable cities.

Monterey became famous as a picturesque sardine cannery town when John Steinbeck published *Cannery Row* in 1945. Though the city of Monterey is now a major tourist attraction, much of the charm captured in his book has been preserved: the commercial wharf where the daily catch is off-loaded from fishing boats; large fishing boats in the harbor adorned with nets, crab traps and huge floats; sidewalk vendors (on Fisherman's Wharf) selling fresh fish, shellfish, squid and hot chowder; the exteriors of the old cannery buildings; and the old adobe buildings dating back to the 1800s, which have been restored to their original condition. Some extraordinary structures, such as the Monterey Bay Aquarium, have been built within the walls of the old cannery buildings.

The city of Carmel (also known as Carmel-by-the-Sea) is south of Monterey on the west side of Carmel Bay and is actually part of the Monterey Peninsula. Carmel is a seaside resort town of charming Victorian bed-and-breakfast inns, quaint shops and quiet coastal drives. Though it once had a reputation as a bohemian retreat, it is now one of Central California's major tourist destinations.

The Big Sur coast is just south of the Monterey Peninsula. Though sparsely populated, this area attracts many divers, hikers and other vacationers seeking both relaxation and adventure within the region's wooded foothills, rocky coastline and underwater terrain.

You'll find Sonoma and Mendocino Counties north of the San Francisco Bay Area, along the ruggedly beautiful coastline. From Jenner north to Gualala, the shoreline consists of grassy meadows and forests that look down on the ocean from high bluffs. The ocean washes up against steep rocky cliffs, broken occasionally by small coves. Nestled in the wooded meadows is what seems to be a never-ending ribbon of bed-and-breakfast inns. In the city of Mendocino, boutiques, restaurants and specialty shops line Main Street, and bustling streams of busy tourists are in constant motion.

# History

Before the European occupation of North America, California was populated by several tribes of Native Americans. These peoples lived in relative isolation as a result of the high mountains to the east, desert to the south and ocean to the west.

In the early 1500s, Spain began colonizing the Americas. By 1602, explorers were charting "Alta California" (what is now the California coast), but the region's first Colonial expedition, the "Sacred Expedition," didn't converge on San Diego until 1769. Spain's goal was to increase its political and religious influence through establishing Catholic missions and military garrisons, with the idea of converting the natives and incorporating them into Spanish culture. Eventually, four presidios were established, at San Diego (1769), Monterey (1770), San Francisco (1776) and Santa Barbara (1782). Attracting Spanish settlers and converting the natives proved to be more difficult than expected, and little progress was made to secure Spain's foothold in this undeveloped land.

When Mexico gained independence from Spain in 1821, the new government regarded the church with mistrust and sought new ways to make California a profitable possession. In 1833 the missions were secularized. Mission lands were appropriated and divided between the mission Indians and new settlers. These *ranchos* became the focal points of a pastoral society that produced huge numbers of cattle, but little else. Trade with outsiders grew out of control during Mexican rule, as American traders bought the hides and sold every necessity and luxury that could be produced on the East Coast and shipped around Cape Horn.

In the early 1800s, American interest in California increased on two levels. Officially, driven by a belief in the "manifest destiny" of the U.S., various offers were made to purchase Alta California from the Mexican government. Unofficially, American explorers, trappers, traders, whalers, settlers and opportunists entered California and seized on many profit-making opportunities that the Mexican Californians ignored in favor of ranching.

Indians, Spaniards, Mexicans, and American Yankees weren't the only occupants of the region at this time. Other settlers included Russian sea-otter hunters who established a fort just north of San Francisco in 1812 (at Fort Ross, in the area still known as the Russian River), and Chinese immigrants who helped build the Central Pacific Railroad network in the mid-1800s.

The reconstructed Fort Ross houses California history displays.

## Steinbeck: Hero or Local Villain?

John Steinbeck was born in Salinas, California, in 1902. He went to Salinas High School and worked as a hired hand on nearby ranches. He studied English at Stanford University off and on between 1919 and 1925, though he did not earn a degree. In 1925 he moved to New York to pursue a writing career, but left the next year before finding a publisher or making a name for himself.

In 1926 he returned to California and lived in Pacific Grove, gathering material for *Tortilla Flat* and *Cannery Row*. *Tortilla Flat* (1935) won the Commonwealth Club's California Book Award Gold Medal for Literature. When *The Grapes of Wrath* (1939) won the Pulitzer Prize, it brought international attention to the living conditions and exploitation of farm workers. However, Steinbeck was vilified for his dark portrayal of many of Monterey Peninsula's prominent landowners and bankers. Though spurned throughout his lifetime by many from his hometown for his controversial writings about the region, Steinbeck was awarded the Nobel Prize for Literature in 1962 and is now considered by many to be one of the United States' most notable novelists. The National Steinbeck Center was founded in 1977 to share Steinbeck's life and work. The Center now presents historical and educational materials and activities from its beautiful Salinas facility, inaugurated in June 1998. For more information, call ☎ 831-796-3833.

American settlers in California became increasingly discontented with the ineffective and remote government in Mexico City. In May 1846, the U.S. declared war on Mexico, and U.S. forces quickly occupied all the presidios and imposed martial law. The Mexicans had little choice but to cede much of their northern territory to the U.S. The Treaty of Guadalupe Hidalgo, signed on February 2, 1848, turned over California to the U.S., along with most of New Mexico and Arizona.

By an amazing coincidence, gold was discovered in Northern California within days of signing the treaty with Mexico. With a characteristically Californian blend of hype and enthusiasm, the gold discovery transformed the new American outpost. The growth and wealth stimulated every aspect of life, from agriculture and banking to construction and journalism, and brought vast numbers of prospectors from all over the world. By 1850 this multicultural territory was admitted to the union as a non-slave state. A progressive constitution was soon established, setting the stage for the state's future as one of the strongest economic forces in the world.

# Diving History

The first divers in the Monterey Peninsula area were deep-sea "hard hat" divers who installed and maintained the underwater pipes that connected floating off-shore hoppers to the sardine canneries. The sardine fleets discharged their catch into the cannery hoppers, 500 to 700ft (150 to 210m) offshore. The canneries would pump the fish from the hoppers, through the pipes and into the canneries for processing. Knut Hovden, original owner of the Hovden Food Products Corporation, developed this system in 1927. (The Hovden cannery building now houses the Monterey Bay Aquarium.) The divers wore bulky dive suits, weighted boots and heavy helmets connected to surface air pumps by rubber hoses. Originally these divers assembled 12ft (4m) sections of steel pipe by bolting them together underwater. In the 1930s, the pipes were welded onshore, but divers were still required to place pipes on the seafloor, as well as to repair damage caused by storms or corrosion.

Sport diving in Northern California began, as in most places, as a macho endeavor driven by the excitement of the unknown and a longing to kill everything that moved. In the early years, little or nothing was known about the "bends," dive tables, nitrogen narcosis or how the laws of physics apply to breathing underwater.

Hard hat divers were the first to explore Monterey Bay.

In the late 1950s a few people dived without protective suits, applying petroleum products (such as Vaseline) for warmth. Divers later cut and glued pieces of rubber in their garages to form poorly fitted dive suits that afforded a bit more protection against the chilly Pacific. Most of these early divers were hunters who fashioned spearguns and pole spears from corrosive metal rods.

In the late '50s, Lloyd Bridges starred in the popular television series *Sea Hunt*, bringing a Hollywood version of underwater California into the homes of millions. His daring exploits inspired many more adventurous souls to fasten double-hosed regulators to air tanks made from surplus oxygen cylinders.

In the '70s, underwater photographers, explorers and sightseers of both sexes began to replace the macho element in the dive industry. As the industry became more safety oriented and the equipment became more user-friendly, dive classes started filling up with men and women. In Monterey, tourists lined the beaches to watch the "men (and women) in black" disappear into the surf. In the late '70s, day boats and six-pack dive boats such as the *Navillus* and the *Monterey Spirit* took divers from Monterey Harbor to new offshore dive sites. Television continued to bring beautiful and exciting images of kelp forests to the masses, and more people wanted to experience this new sport for themselves.

Interest in exploring California's coastal waters has increased over the years. The advent of single-hosed regulators such as the Aqua-Lung (marketed in the '60s) and such startling innovations as horse collar BCs, pre-made black rubber wetsuits and pressure gauges—as well as the dive stores to rent and sell these innovations—has made sport diving in California and elsewhere safer and more accessible to the general population. Tens of thousands of Californians are certified each year. Today, with the invention and ensuing popularity of drysuits, divers can explore the mysteries of the deep while staying comfortably warm.

While better technology has made diving safer and easier, increased pressures on the marine ecosystem have changed the face of diving over the years. Fish that once were seen in schools of thousands now are seen only in the hundreds. Gill nets, heavy commercial fishing, live fish fisheries and the El Niño weather system anomaly have had a large impact on fish populations. However, the numbers of fish are now so low that any taking (even by sport divers) presents a serious problem. Though red abalone are still plentiful on the north coast in deeper water (below 15ft or 4.6m) and in harder-to-access areas, commercial take and poaching have dealt heavy blows to the abalone population, especially in the shallow areas. In Southern California, diseases like withering syndrome have also attacked the ab population. In response to these pressures, regulations were established to protect many coastal and marine areas, as well as specific marine species, though they are not always consistently enforced or effective.

Drysuits and other innovations make cold-water diving more comfortable.

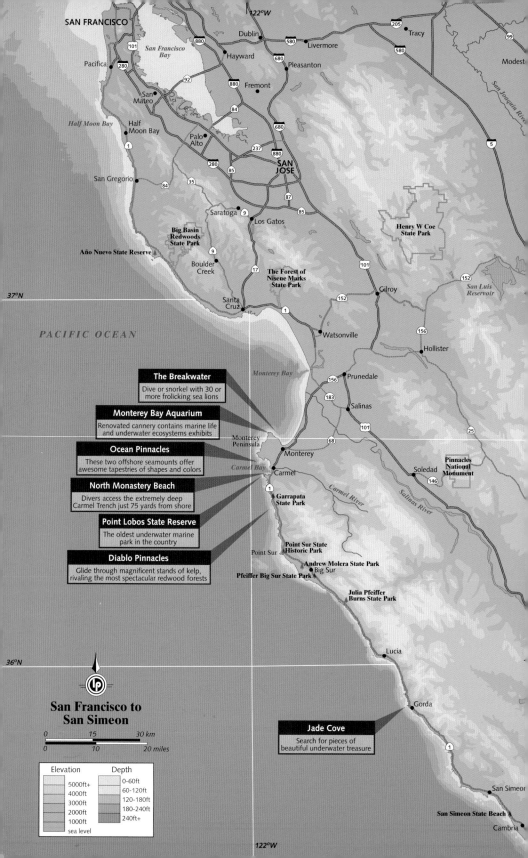

SAN FRANCISCO

122°W

Tracy

205

99

Dublin

Modesto

580

Livermore

Pacifica

101

San Francisco Bay

880

Hayward

680

Pleasanton

580

280

92

San Mateo

880

Fremont

San Joaquin River

Half Moon Bay

Half Moon Bay

84

5

1

Palo Alto

680

San Gregorio

280

237

SAN JOSE

84

35

85

87

Saratoga

9

Los Gatos

85

Henry W Coe State Park

Big Basin Redwoods State Park

152

San Luis Reservoir

Año Nuevo State Reserve

9

Boulder Creek

The Forest of Nisene Marks State Park

101

Gilroy

152

37°N

Santa Cruz

17

1

152

156

Hollister

**PACIFIC OCEAN**

Watsonville

Monterey Bay

156

Prunedale

**The Breakwater**
Dive or snorkel with 30 or more frolicking sea lions

183

Salinas

25

**Monterey Bay Aquarium**
Renovated cannery contains marine life and underwater ecosystems exhibits

101

**Ocean Pinnacles**
These two offshore seamounts offer awesome tapestries of shapes and colors

Monterey Peninsula

68

**Pinnacles National Monument**

Monterey

**North Monastery Beach**
Divers access the extremely deep Carmel Trench just 75 yards from shore

Carmel Bay

Carmel

Soledad

146

Salinas River

1

Garrapata State Park

Carmel River

**Point Lobos State Reserve**
The oldest underwater marine park in the country

**Diablo Pinnacles**
Glide through magnificent stands of kelp, rivaling the most spectacular redwood forests

Point Sur State Historic Park

Point Sur

Andrew Molera State Park

Big Sur

Pfeiffer Big Sur State Park

Julia Pfeiffer Burns State Park

Lucia

36°N

Gorda

**San Francisco to San Simeon**

0        15        30 km

0        10        20 miles

**Jade Cove**
Search for pieces of beautiful underwater treasure

1

Elevation

5000ft+
4000ft
3000ft
2000ft
1000ft
sea level

Depth

0-60ft
60-120ft
120-180ft
180-240ft
240ft+

San Simeon

San Simeon State Beach

Cambria

122°W

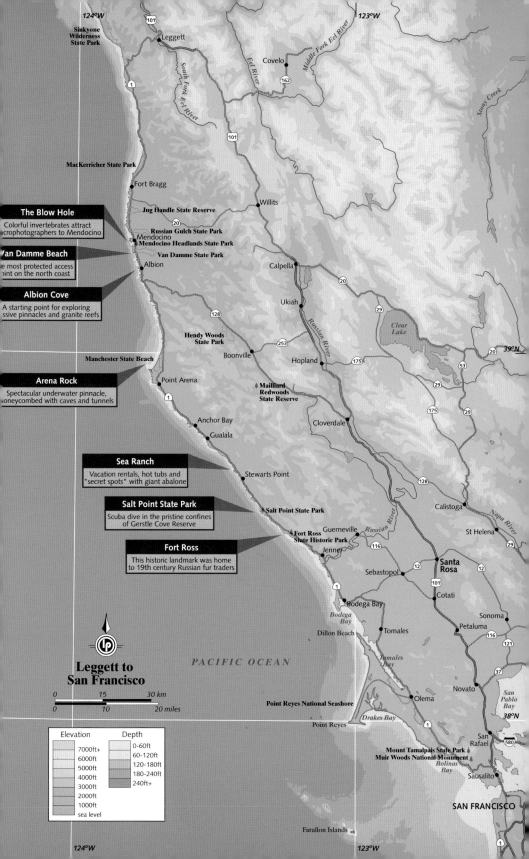

Sinkyone
Wilderness
State Park

124°W

123°W

101 Leggett

Covelo

*Eel River*

*Middle Fork Eel River*

162

*South Fork Eel River*

1

*Stony Creek*

101

MacKerricher State Park

Fort Bragg

Willits

Jug Handle State Reserve

**The Blow Hole**
Colorful invertebrates attract
acrophotographers to Mendocino

20

Russian Gulch State Park
Mendocino
Mendocino Headlands State Park

Calpella

**Van Damme Beach**
e most protected access
oint on the north coast

Van Damme State Park

Albion

20

**Albion Cove**
A starting point for exploring
ssive pinnacles and granite reefs

128

Ukiah

29

*Clear Lake*

Hendy Woods
State Park

253

20

39°N

53

Manchester State Beach

Boonville

Hopland

175

**Arena Rock**
Spectacular underwater pinnacle,
oneycombed with caves and tunnels

Point Arena

1

Mailliard
Redwoods
State Reserve

29

175

29

Anchor Bay

Gualala

*Russian River*

Cloverdale

**Sea Ranch**
Vacation rentals, hot tubs and
"secret spots" with giant abalone

Stewarts Point

128

Calistoga

*Napa River*

**Salt Point State Park**
Scuba dive in the pristine confines
of Gerstle Cove Reserve

Salt Point State Park

Guerneville

*Russian River*

St Helena

29

**Fort Ross**
This historic landmark was home
to 19th century Russian fur traders

Fort Ross
State Historic Park

Jenner

116

Santa
Rosa

12

Sebastopol

12

Cotati

101

Sonoma

**Leggett to
San Francisco**

Bodega Bay

*Bodega Bay*

Petaluma

116

121

Dillon Beach

Tomales

37

*PACIFIC OCEAN*

*Tomales Bay*

Novato

*San Pablo Bay*

0      15      30 km
0      10      20 miles

Point Reyes National Seashore

Olema

38°N

580

*Drakes Bay*

1

San
Rafael

Point Reyes

| Elevation | Depth |
|---|---|
| 7000ft+ | 0-60ft |
| 6000ft | 60-120ft |
| 5000ft | 120-180ft |
| 4000ft | 180-240ft |
| 3000ft | 240ft+ |
| 2000ft | |
| 1000ft | |
| sea level | |

Mount Tamalpais State Park
Muir Woods National Monument
*Bolinas Bay*

Sausalito

**SAN FRANCISCO**

Farallon Islands

1

124°W

123°W

# Practicalities

## Climate

Central and Northern California's coastal weather is quite different from the warm, sunny weather found nearly year-round at Southern California's beaches. Though the weather is moderate—averaging in the high 40s in January to the mid 60s in August—it is rarely predictable and only generally follows seasonal patterns. During the spring and summer months, the normal forecast is for fog that burns off by late morning or early afternoon. Fall and winter are often drizzly and overcast, and storms are likely to hit the coast, but you may experience beautiful sunny days even during this time of year. When planning a trip, always check the weekly forecast.

## Water Temperature

California water temperatures are affected by a number of factors, including depth and currents. Surface temperatures usually range from 48 to 56°F (9 to 13°C). The temperatures stay fairly constant down to 30 to 40ft (10 to 12m). You will often encounter significantly colder temperatures in deeper water—as low as 45°F (7°C)—due to thermoclines or deepwater upwelling. Occasionally, warm currents from the south (called El Niño currents) warm the surface temperatures by as much as 15°F (8°C) for short periods of time. Most local divers wear a minimum quarter-inch (7mm) wetsuit to protect themselves against the cold. Drysuits, which help keep divers warmer for long periods of time, have become very popular among local sport divers.

## El Niño

Most years, the water temperature along the Central and Northern California coast changes very little throughout the year. Every three to seven years, water temperatures increase dramatically along the coast of South America, caused by the climatic phenomenon known as El Niño. The warm waters travel northward in a current called the El Niño current. During El Niño years, water temperatures in Central California can climb to balmy heights, sometimes reaching more than 60°F (16°C). The warmer waters bring fish and animals that are usually found only much farther south. Sheephead, pelagic red crabs, marlin and even a few spiny lobsters have been found as far north as Monterey. Some of these visitors, such as sheephead, have become permanent residents in this area. Not all the effects of El Niño are positive. This phenomenon can also cause droughts and severe winter storms.

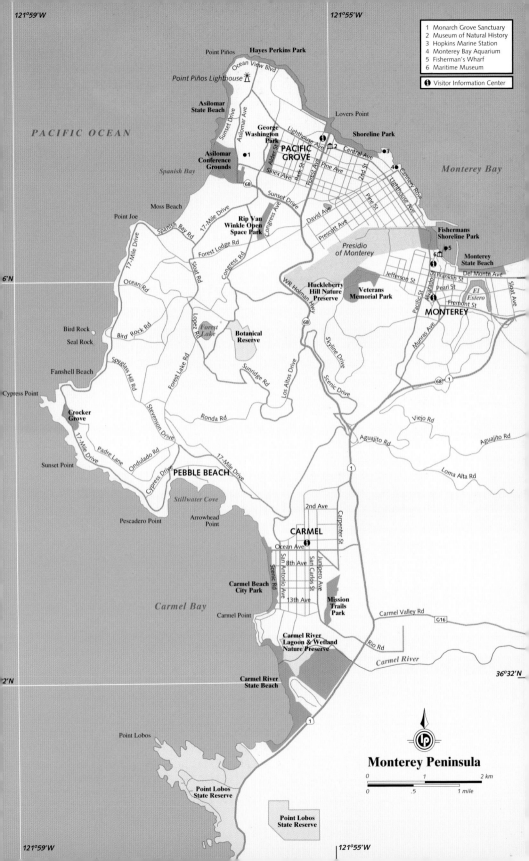

**Monterey Peninsula**

# Getting There

The San Francisco Bay Area is the major transportation hub for travelers to the Central and Northern California coast. The San Francisco, San Jose and Oakland International Airports are the three major airports serving the Bay Area, and each has connecting flights to the Monterey Airport.

# Getting Around

Most divers opt to drive to the various dive regions because of the bulky and heavy gear necessary for California diving, the lack of convenient public transportation, the expense of flying and the reasonably short driving distances. For those who do fly to the area, rental cars are readily available at the major airports.

The most direct way to drive from the Bay Area to Monterey and coastal points south is to take Highway 101 south from San Jose, then take Highway 156 west to Highway 1, and continue south on Highway 1. The city of Monterey is approximately 72 miles (116km) from San Jose, Carmel is 4 miles (6km) farther south, and Big Sur is 38 miles (61km) south of Monterey.

There are several ways to drive to Northern California coastal dive sites. You can choose either a winding scenic route or a faster (and still fairly scenic) route to most sites.

To reach Jenner (the jumping off point for Sonoma coast dive sites) from San Francisco, take Highway 101 to the Russian River/Old River Road turnoff just north of Santa Rosa. (Santa Rosa is approximately 55 miles from San

## Monterey Parking Tips

There is plenty of convenient parking near the dive sites on the Monterey Peninsula. Keep a few basic tips in mind to make parking as hassle-free as possible:

**Arrive Early** If you are diving at a popular beach dive location or in an area where there is heavy tourist traffic, try to arrive before 9am to get a good space.

**Bring Quarters** If you will be parking in one of the fee lots, remember to take lots of quarters to feed the ticket machine. Always pay for more time than you anticipate using for the dive. Invariably, you will run into an old dive buddy or make new friends with whom you will wind up swapping stories about your dives. Either that or you will forget a piece of gear and make an extra trip or two between the car and the beach. Don't forget to place the parking stubs in plain view on the left-hand side of your dashboard.

**Know the Rules** Whether you park in a lot or on the street, make sure you know what regulations and time limits apply. Parking tickets are a great source of revenue and all parking areas are frequently monitored.

**Spare Key** It is always a good idea to keep a spare car key with you in a safe place.

Francisco.) The Old River Road joins Highway 116 at Guerneville and continues west to Jenner and the coast. The road from Guerneville to Jenner borders the Russian River, which provides beautiful riparian scenery for the drive. You can also reach Jenner by taking Highway 101 to the Bodega Bay/East Washington exit in Petaluma. (Petaluma is approximately 39 miles from San Francisco.) This scenic country farm route is slightly slower and joins Highway 1 just below Bodega Bay after about a 28-mile drive. Jenner is 10 miles (16km) farther north.

Most of the dive sites along the Mendocino coast are at the northern end of the county. There are two main routes to the Mendocino coast by car. You can continue north on Highway 1 from the Sonoma coast, but the drive is slow and winding. If drive time is an issue, take Highway 101 north to Cloverdale, where Highway 128 cuts west across to Highway 1 on the coast. This route can save up to two hours driving time from the San Francisco Bay Area. (Cloverdale is approximately 88 miles north of San Francisco.) The distance between Cloverdale and Highway 1 is approximately 56 miles (90km) of winding country road.

# Time

California is on Pacific Standard Time and, like most of the rest of the U.S., observes daylight saving time. When it is noon in California, it is 3pm in New York, 8pm in London and 7am the following day in Sydney.

# What to Bring

## General Supplies

Accessibility of general supplies and gas varies considerably along the California coast. On the Monterey Peninsula, most dive sites are located in the cities of Monterey, Pacific Grove or Carmel, which have plenty of places to get gas and provisions. The dive sites along the Big Sur coast are more remote and there are few on-shore facilities, so you have to take everything with you and make sure that you have plenty of fuel. There are a couple of gas stations and convenience stores (at Big Sur Center south of Point Sur, and at Gorda south of Jade Cove), but they are not always open.

In Sonoma County between Jenner and Stewart's Point there are several small grocery stores where you can purchase sundries and snacks (Jenner, Fort Ross, Timber Cove, Ocean Cove and Stewart's Point). In Mendocino County there is a large grocery store in Gualala (at the southern end of Mendocino County), and a number of stores between Navarro and Mendocino where you can pick up snacks, provisions and sundries. The most touristed area of Mendocino County is the northern city of Mendocino, which has several stores and gas stations. Fort Bragg (the largest city on the north coast) boasts a large grocery store, many other shops and restaurants, gas stations, a movie theater, etc.

Because the weather along the California coast is variable and daily temperature changes can be drastic, it is always a good idea to bring a range of clothing. Even in the summer months, the coast is often foggy and damp in the mornings and then warm and sunny in the afternoons. It is a good idea to pack a warm jacket as well as a T-shirt and shorts. In the fall and winter months it gets downright chilly and warm clothing is essential.

Other general supplies that you should consider packing are a basic first-aid kit, a plastic tub for wet dive gear, a plastic tub or cooler (and plastic garbage bags) if free-diving for abalone, a tarp to put on the ground to minimize dirt and sand on wet dive gear when you are changing, towels for showers at the dive shops before the trip home, and lots of quarters for the parking meters and parking ticket machines.

## Dive-Related Equipment

Though the weather varies daily, the water temperature changes very little during the year. It is always cold, requiring substantial thermal protection. A quarter-inch (7mm) wetsuit is minimal, and a drysuit is a better option (for scuba diving, not for free-diving). Most dive stores on the Monterey Peninsula stock an excellent range of rental equipment, including wetsuits, weight belts, tanks, regulators and gauges, buoyancy compensators, masks, fins and extras. Many have not only added drysuit rentals to their inventories, but also offer free or very reasonable familiarization courses or seminars in the use of drysuits. Many dive shops along the Monterey Peninsula also offer nitrox (enriched air mixtures) airfills. For busy weekends, it is advisable to call and reserve what you need in advance.

On the north coast there are dive shops in Fort Bragg, Albion and Gualala where you can rent gear, but you should check availability in advance. A few other places offer limited equipment such as ab gauges and ab irons. Fishing licenses are available at most convenience stores up and down the coast (in Sonoma County at Jenner, Fort Ross and Ocean Cove; in Mendocino County at Albion, Little River, Mendocino and Fort Bragg).

# Underwater Photography

Underwater photography is a popular diving activity in California. Several shops sell underwater photography gear, though rental gear is not as common. **Backscatter**, at the breakwater in Monterey, has rental gear. See the Listings section for details. There are several places that offer E6 processing and, of course, print processing in the Monterey area: **Bay Photo Lab** (763 Lighthouse Ave., Monterey ☎ 831-372-6337), **Fry Photographics** (251 Pearl St., Monterey ☎ 831-655-4941), and **Green's Camera World** (472 Alvarado St., Monterey ☎ 831-655-1234; 213 Forest Ave., Pacific Grove ☎ 831-373-3686; Ocean Ave. between San Carlos and Mission, Carmel ☎ 831-625-9066).

# Tips & Tricks for Underwater Photography

California diving offers incredible video and photo opportunities. The nutritive cold waters support an awesome variety of colorful and exciting subjects. However, because of the limited visibility, poor ambient light and surge, this area poses more underwater photography challenges than clear, warm-water destinations. The possible results are worth the effort.

Simplicity is one of the best recommendations for taking pictures in these conditions. Simplify your equipment and simplify your subject selection. The more compact your camera setup is, the less it will be pushed around by the surge. This also cuts down on the likelihood of getting your camera and strobes entangled in the kelp.

Because you are primarily—sometimes solely—using artificial light, backscatter (the reflection of light off particles in the water column) is a major obstacle. Sidelight your subject and aim your flash so that the nearest angle of the beam illuminates the subject, not the water column between the lens and the subject. This will help minimize the effects of backscatter. Try handholding a single strobe to give you the most flexibility in any situation.

Water turbidity can cause images to lose their sharpness. The more water there is between your lens and the subject, the softer or fuzzier the image will appear. For each subject, select a lens that allows you to get as close to your subject as possible, giving you a full-frame shot. If you are shooting wide-angle, concentrate on focusing and lighting a subject near you. Shoot the balance of the picture in ambient light. If you are shooting close-up or macrophotography, fill the frame with your subject and select an uncluttered background.

If you concentrate on shooting a single subject, it is easier to compose, focus and expose your subject. Because there are so many variables, it is always helpful to bracket with multiple exposures and flash angles.

Maintenance is very important, especially when you are beach diving. Sand has a way of getting onto everything, including o-rings. Make sure that you soak your cameras and strobes in fresh water as soon as possible after the dive. Also, clean and grease every o-ring you can get to after each dive.

# Accommodations

Countless accommodations options exist along California's coast. Regional tourism offices, the state park system and private campgrounds are useful resources when looking for appropriate places to stay on your dive vacation. See the Listings section for details.

Monterey and Carmel offer a variety of places to stay in a range of budgets. However, these are popular tourist towns and there are so many things going on that rooms often fill up far in advance. Make reservations if you know ahead of time when you will be diving. Rates during the week are usually less expensive than on weekends.

The Big Sur coast offers several campgrounds and well-known spas and inns. There is a motel in Big Sur and several places that have cabins, but none would be considered budget accommodations.

In Sonoma County, there are many campgrounds along the coast, as well as a few motels and lodges scattered between Jenner and Stewart's Point. One of the campgrounds, Timber Cove, also has home and cabin rentals. Another option is for small groups or a couple of families to share a rental property at Sea Ranch, at the north end of Sonoma County.

Mendocino County has a surprising number of motels, lodges and bed-and-breakfast inns scattered along its scenic coastline. The stretch of coastline from Navarro River to Cleone, north of Fort Bragg, is something of a "bed-and-breakfast row," and there are also several nice campgrounds. Visitors will find a laundry list of fabulous places to stay, though few would be considered budget accommodations. However, prices can be considerably less expensive if you make a reservation in advance for stays during the week or in rooms that don't have views. Ask about specials before booking. Although accommodations may seem plentiful, it can be difficult to find a hotel or motel room, camper hookups or space at a campsite, especially on weekends. Make your reservations early, and check on the weather and water conditions before you head north.

Many old Victorians are now B&Bs.

# Dining & Food

There is no end to the variety of restaurants available in California. The Monterey Peninsula, between the productive and fertile Salinas Valley and the bountiful Pacific Ocean, never lacks fresh vegetables or seafood. Of course, seafood restaurants, featuring calamari, clam chowder, ahi and albacore tuna, scallops and crab dishes, are probably the most popular restaurants with visitors to the area. These restaurants draw from a long and tasty culinary tradition, influenced by Italian immigrants, fishermen and California produce. There are also excellent French restaurants, Mexican restaurants, sushi bars, and restaurants specializing in California cuisine. Price-wise, the options are many.

North of San Francisco there are a number of roadside diners along Highway 1, and a variety of options, including fine dining, is available in the larger cities such as Bodega Bay, Jenner, Gualala, Mendocino and Fort Bragg. You can also get a decent meal at Timber Cove Lodge and Salt Point Lodge.

## What's for Dinner?

Increased consumer demand and poor fishing practices are detrimental to the populations of many fish species worldwide. The choices you make when buying seafood at local restaurants and stores can have an impact on their survival. The following species have been overfished and their populations drastically reduced. You can avoid contributing to their decline by not purchasing them.

### Avoid:

Bluefin tuna

Lingcod

Rockfish/pacific
red snapper/rock cod

Sablefish/butterfish/
black cod

Shark (any kind)

Swordfish

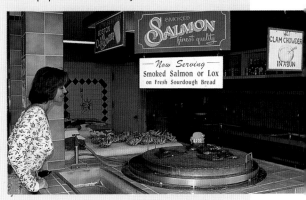

Monterey is synonymous with delicious seafood.

For more information about selecting seafood, contact the Audubon Living Oceans Program, which publishes the Audubon Seafood Lover's Almanac, at www. audubon.org.

# Activities & Attractions

The list of activities and attractions along Central and Northern California's coast is seemingly endless. Outdoor enthusiasts will enjoy walking and hiking along the beaches, coastal mountain ranges, pygmy forests and fern grottos. Biking, boating and fishing are also popular options, and rental equipment is available in many locations. If time permits, you'll undoubtedly want to tour one of the nearby wineries, go whale watching, or simply browse a few of the quaint shops that line the streets of many coastal towns. The following list includes just a few of the highlights that shouldn't be missed.

## Monterey Bay Aquarium

The historic Hovden cannery building at the northwest end of Cannery Row is now home to the Monterey Bay Aquarium. The Aquarium is a nonprofit, self

The Monterey Bay Aquarium has become an eye-appealing landmark for divers.

supporting institution whose mission is to inspire conservation of the oceans. Aquarium exhibits represent a living extension of Monterey Bay—the centerpiece of the nation's largest national marine sanctuary. The largest display is the "kelp forest" tank, which towers 28ft (8.5m) high, extends 90ft (28m) long and holds 335,000 gallons (1,268 cubic meters) of seawater. This exhibit offers you a window into a saltwater kelp forest without getting wet. A second tank, only slightly smaller, houses "Monterey Bay Habitats," where you can observe sharks, salmon, halibut, striped bass and other marine creatures amid deep reefs, sandy bottoms, shale shoals and 30-year-old pilings from a Monterey wharf. "Mysteries of the Deep," a display that opened in 1996 and will run through January 2002, presents more than 40 species collected from the depths of Monterey's submarine canyon. Other exhibits include the marine-mammal educational area, the bat ray pool and the touch tank. The aquarium is at 886 Cannery Row. For more information, call ☎ 831-648-4800, or look at their website at www.mbayaq.org.

# 17-Mile Drive

The scenic 17-Mile Drive through the private community of Pebble Beach (between Monterey and Carmel) takes you along some of the most beautiful and fascinating shoreline in the world. The picturesque views encompass rocky outcroppings, wind-ravaged cypress trees and crashing waves. Where the surf is calm, the diving can be exceptional. Cypress Point and Stillwater Cove both have easy-to-access shore entries. Harbor seals and sea lions perch atop offshore rocks. Squadrons of brown pelicans glide in formation inches from the surface of the water. Hundreds of mansions dot the hills alongside the road. The $7.50 per vehicle admission price includes access to the beaches and hiking trails in the area. There are five gated entry points into this private community, all of which link up with the drive.

# Point Lobos State Reserve

The reserve, with its dramatically rocky and convoluted coastline, takes its name from the *Punta de los Lobos Marinos*, or the "Point of the Sea Wolves," named by the Spanish for the howls of the resident sea lions. Point Lobos encompasses 554 land acres as well as 750 submerged acres that are good for scuba diving. There's a terrific selection of short walks, most of them less than a mile long, which take you through the wild and inspiring scenery. Favorite destinations include Sea Lion Point and Devil's Cauldron, the latter a blowhole and whirlpool that gets splashy at high tide.

The reserve entrance is on the west side of Highway 1, about 4 miles south of Carmel. It's open 9am to 7pm daily (to 5pm in winter); $7 per vehicle, free for walk-ins. For more information, call ☎ 831-624-4909, or look at their website at www.pt-lobos.parks.state.ca.us.

# Whale-Watching Tours

Gray whales can be seen along the California coastline from December through April as they migrate from the cold waters of Alaska to the warm lagoons on the west coast of Mexico's Baja California peninsula and then return. Several operators run charter boats from Monterey Harbor, and there are a couple of whale charters out of Fort Bragg, but no licensed dive charters. Dive Crazy (out of Albion along the Mendocino coast) will do whale-watching, fishing and dive charters. From June through October, blue, orca, humpback and minke whales, as well as dolphins, can be seen in the Monterey Bay Sanctuary. A three- to four-hour boat tour will give you the best chance to see one of these magnificent cetaceans.

Rental kayaks are a great way to observe marine life.

# Kayaking

For an up-close and personal look at some of Monterey's fascinating otters, seals or sea lions, rent a kayak and paddle off to adventure. The best places to rent kayaks are the Elkhorn Slough at Moss Landing, Del Monte Beach adjacent to Wharf #2 or at the Breakwater adjacent to the boat ramps. Several companies rent kayaks for about $25 a day. Remember that you are required to stay at least 50ft from marine mammals unless they initiate contact.

On the north coast, kayak rentals are available at Van Damme State Park and at the Dive Crazy dive shop at Schooner's Landing in Albion. The coves along the coast to the south of Van Damme are spectacular. There are tunnels that you can paddle through (only when it is calm), incredible rock formations, harbor seals and gorgeous scenery.

# Fort Ross State Historic Park

Just 11 miles north of Jenner on Highway 1 you'll find Fort Ross, the southern-most American outpost of the 19th-century Russian fur trade. In March 1812, a group of 25 Russians and 80 Native Alaskans from the Kodiak, Kenai and Aleutian tribes arrived and began to build the wooden fort at Fort Ross, near the site of Meteni, a Kashaya Pomo Indian village. The fort was established as a base for sea otter hunting operations, for growing wheat and other crops to supply Russian settlements in Alaska and as a base for trade with Spanish Alta California. The Russians dedicated the fort on August 13, 1812, and occupied it until 1842, abandoning it because the sea otter population had been decimated and the agricultural production was never as great as hoped.

Fort Ross today is an accurate historical reconstruction of the Russian fort; only one building is original. Most of the original construction was sold, dismantled and carried away to Sutter's Fort in California's Central Valley during the gold rush.

The fort is open daily 10am to 4:30pm; $6 per vehicle. The visitor center (☎ 707-847-3286) has good displays on the history of the fort and an excellent library on California history, nature and other topics. On Living History Day, held the last Saturday in July, costumed volunteers bring the fort's history back to life.

Fort Ross occupies a prominent location overlooking the ocean.

# Diving Health & Safety

## General Overview

California is generally a healthy and safe place to travel. There are no prevalent diseases or risks associated with traveling here. In the case of a diving or other injury, medical and emergency facilities are accessible throughout the state. Most health risks associated with diving are easy to prevent or avoid. In the water, use adequate protection against the cold, and always be careful entering and exiting rocky shore dives. Out of the water, be sure to use sunscreen and drink plenty of fluids.

### DAN

Divers Alert Network (DAN) is an international membership association of individuals and organizations sharing a common interest in diving and safety. It operates a 24-hour diving emergency hotline in the U.S.: ☎ 919-684-8111 or 919-684-4DAN (-4326). The latter accepts collect calls in a dive emergency. Though DAN does not directly provide medical care, it does provide advice on early treatment, evacuation and hyperbaric treatment of diving-related injuries. Divers should contact DAN for assistance as soon as a diving emergency is suspected.

DAN membership is reasonably priced and includes DAN TravelAssist, a membership benefit that covers medical air evacuation from anywhere in the world for any illness or injury. For a small additional fee, divers can get secondary insurance coverage for decompression illness. For membership questions, contact DAN at ☎ 800-446-2671 in the U.S. or ☎ 919-684-2948 elsewhere. DAN can also be reached at www.diversalertnetwork.org.

## Pre-Trip Preparation

Your general state of health, diving skill level and specific equipment needs are the three most important factors that impact any dive trip. If you honestly assess these before diving, you'll be well on your way to assuring a safe dive trip.

First, if you're not in shape, start exercising. Second, if you haven't dived for a while (six months is too long) and your skills are rusty, select an easy beach or boat dive and dive with an experienced buddy, or take a scuba review course. Finally, inspect your dive gear with enough anticipation that you can make other arrangements should you find a problem. Remember, your regulator should be serviced annually, whether you've used it or not. If you use a dive computer and can replace the battery yourself, change it before the trip or buy a spare one to take along. Otherwise, send the computer to the manufacturer for a battery replacement.

Do a final check of your gear, grease o-rings and assemble a save-a-dive kit. This kit should at minimum contain extra mask and fin straps, snorkel keeper, mouthpiece, valve cap, zip ties and o-rings. A spare mask is also a good idea. Purchase or arrange to rent any additional equipment, such as a dive light and tank marker light for night diving, etc. Make sure you have at least a whistle attached to your BC. Better yet, add a marker tube (also known as a safety sausage or come-to-me). Don't forget to pack a first-aid kit and medications such as decongestants, ear drops, antihistamines and seasickness tablets. Feeling good physically, and diving with experience and with reliable equipment will not only increase your safety, but will also enhance your enjoyment underwater.

# Recompression & Medical Facilities

For central coast divers who may be experiencing decompression sickness symptoms, contact the Community Hospital of the Monterey Peninsula on Highway 68 (☎ 831-624-5311 or emergency medical services ☎ 831-625-4900). They will make a referral to the Pacific Grove Fire Department's two-person recompression chamber (600 Pine Avenue at Forest Avenue in Pacific Grove). The chamber is operated by volunteers in conjunction with the Pacific Grove Fire Rescue Service.

North coast divers should call ☎ 911 or DAN in a dive emergency.

For general medical care, there are a number of medical facilities along the California coast. The following are nearest to dive sites:

**Community Hospital of the Monterey Peninsula**
☎ 831-624-5311
23625 Holman Hwy (Highway 68)
Monterey, CA 93940

**Redwood Coast Medical Services**
☎ 707-884-4005 or 707-785-2315
46900 Ocean View Dr.
Gualala, CA 95445

**Mendocino Coast District Hospital**
☎ 707-961-1234
700 River Dr.
Fort Bragg, CA 95437

## Emergency Phone Numbers

For any emergency, call U.S. emergency operator: ☎ 911

Divers Alert Network (DAN): ☎ 919-684-4326

Monterey U.S. Coast Guard: ☎ 831-647-7300

Monterey Group Search and Rescue: ☎ 831-647-7300

Pacific Grove Marine Rescue Patrol: ☎ 831-648-3110

Sonoma County Search and Rescue: ☎ 707-565-2121 (dispatch)

Mendocino County Search and Rescue: ☎ 707-463-4086 (dispatch)

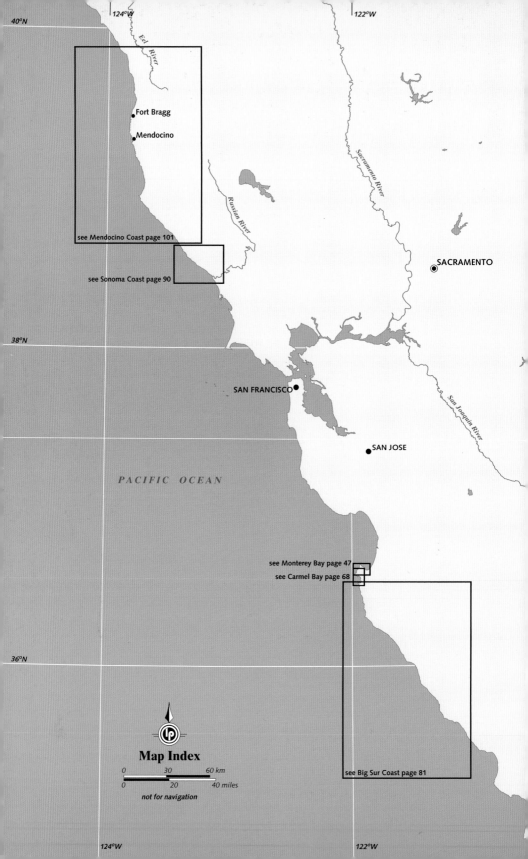

40°N

124°W

122°W

*Eel River*

see Mendocino Coast page 101

• Fort Bragg

• Mendocino

*Russian River*

see Sonoma Coast page 90

*Sacramento River*

⊙ SACRAMENTO

38°N

SAN FRANCISCO ●

SAN JOSE

*San Joaquin River*

*PACIFIC   OCEAN*

see Monterey Bay page 47

see Carmel Bay page 68

36°N

see Big Sur Coast page 81

**Map Index**

| 0 | 30 | 60 km |
| 0 | 20 | 40 miles |

*not for navigation*

124°W

122°W

# Diving in Northern California

Majestic rock formations, marine mammals, vast underwater kelp forests and an array of colorful invertebrates and other marine animals await you in the waters along the Central and Northern California coast. Diving in California is much different than diving in warm-water locales. The hard coral reef formations found in tropical dive destinations don't exist here. California "reef" systems consist of rocky bottoms overgrown with encrusting algae and sponges, anemones and many forms of fast-growing kelp plants. Several species of kelp grow from the rocky substrate and provide habitats for teeming communities of fish, invertebrates and mammals, which live on the seafloor, in the mid-water around the kelp stalks and in the canopy.

## Diving Along the Monterey Peninsula & Central Coast

The Monterey Peninsula, from Del Monte Beach in Monterey Bay to the Point Lobos State Reserve at the southern end of Carmel Bay, is by far the most popular

Hydrocorals are among the many colorful invertebrates found in Monterey.

dive area in Central and Northern California. If you've never dived the area's magnificent kelp forests or explored its underwater canyons, it's understandable that you'd wonder why so many divers enthusiastically jump into water that's 50°F (10°C). The beauty and excitement of diving here far outweigh the hassle of dealing with erratic surf, the cold water temperatures and the inconvenience of a full wetsuit or drysuit. The waters may be chilly compared to warmer climes, but there are sights that warm-water enthusiasts rarely witness: playful sea lions and harbor seals, sea otters that look like teddy bears, majestic birds swooping from the sky, incredible kelp forests and colorful reefs are just a few of the attractions.

Here, most diving is done from the shore. Beach diving, where some amount of surf is the rule, requires special skills. If you're visiting Monterey for the first time, limit your initial dives to areas where the entries and exits are well protected. It is always a good idea to talk with local divers and, if possible, find a dive buddy who is familiar with the area. Local dive stores offer underwater tours led by experienced local divers.

The Monterey Peninsula offers so many tourist attractions that traffic and beach use is heavy. As a result, many local municipalities have passed ordinances restricting parking, gearing up and beach-related activities. Also be aware that many of the dive locations, including parts of Pacific Grove, Hopkins Reef and Point Lobos, are marine reserves where all plants and animals are protected. Local dive stores can brief you on Fish and Game regulations, as well as weather, surf and visibility conditions.

In some areas of Monterey, dive access is regulated because of competing uses.

The Big Sur coast, south of Point Lobos along the central coast, also has some colorful and exciting dive sites. Here you will find diving conditions and marine life similar to the Monterey Peninsula; however, because of the difficult shore access, most Big Sur sites are done as boat dives.

Diving is enjoyed throughout the year along the Monterey Peninsula and the central coast. The fall and winter months, when plankton growth is the lowest, usually provide the best visibility. Though the climate is moderate for most of the year, there is no way of forecasting the dive conditions on any given day. The average visibility in Monterey Bay is 20 to 40ft (6 to 12m), with visibility sometimes exceeding 60ft (18m) along the outer reefs from northern Carmel Bay down to Point Sur, and in the Point Lobos State Reserve, on the southern edge of Carmel Bay.

# Diving Along the North Coast

The north coast of California is perhaps the most scenic coastal region in the world. Grassy meadows, dense redwood and pine forests, and enormous waves pounding against majestic cliffs create a picturesque scene. Though the coast may be beautiful, its diving conditions can be capricious, changing overnight. One day, calm winds and moderate surge invite sport divers to explore its underwater beauty. The next day, the same area can scare off even the most adventurous diver. Sudden swells, crashing waves and powerful wind and rain show the inhospitable side of the north coast. But despite these periods of inclement weather, the coast continues to allure scuba divers and free-divers.

Along the north coast, the dive season is determined not so much by the water conditions (though water temperature and visibility do have an effect) but by the fishing seasons. Abalone diving and spearfishing are the two most popular diving activities in this region. Abalone diving on the north coast is restricted to April through June and August through November. Most of the organized spearfishing events occur during the spring and summer months. However, as more and more scuba divers explore the north coast, they are discovering that some of the more remote offshore reefs and pinnacles are just as colorful and exciting as the best sites on the central coast.

# Diving with Sea Otters, Sea Lions & Harbor Seals

There are several marine mammals that divers often see around the Monterey Peninsula, and may occasionally encounter farther north. Many of these animals are curious and will approach divers, though they can sometimes be aggressive. Be respectful of their territory and do not approach them unless they initiate contact. If and when they do, you are likely to have the dive of a lifetime.

## The California Sea Otter

This creature is one of the most delightful and fascinating attractions of the Monterey Peninsula. Smaller than most other mammals that inhabit these waters, otters measure only 4½ft (1.5m) long. Males weigh approximately 60lbs (27kg), and females weigh about 40lbs (18kg). Unlike sea lions and harbor seals, otters do not have an insulating layer of fat. They keep warm via a layer of air bubbles trapped in their fur, and by

Mother otters are very protective of their pups.

their rapid metabolism. To maintain a high metabolic rate, otters must eat approximately 25% of their body weight every day. Their diet consists of more than 40 kinds of invertebrates, including snails, sea stars, sea urchins, clams, crab, abalone and squid.

Sea otters are often observed in and around kelp beds throughout the Monterey area. They divide their time between sleeping, eating and grooming. Although divers cannot approach them because of their protected status, young male otters will frequently initiate encounters. There are endless stories of otters running off with dive floats or playfully chewing on air hoses and camera cords.

## The California Sea Lion

Sea lions can easily be distinguished from harbor seals: Sea lions have external ear flaps and, on

land, their rear flippers point forward. Bulls weigh as much as 700lbs (318kg) and can reach a length of 10ft (3m). Mature females are much smaller, weighing up to 250lbs (114kg) and rarely reaching 8ft (2.5m) long.

California sea lions are most often found in a rookery (a coastal region occupied by a breeding population) or at a haul-out site (an area occupied by nonbreeding populations). They are very gregarious, usually gathering in groups. The Coast Guard Breakwater in Monterey is a haul-out site where large numbers of sea lions congregate in the nonbreeding season, roughly August through April. Most of the sea lions found at the breakwater are pups and "teenagers," although many large bulls are also present.

Sea lions are a delight to dive with. Younger sea lions are usually very curious about divers and are more than happy to include divers in their enthusiastic play. They will frequently play "chicken," swimming directly at a diver and then blowing bubbles or nipping at a mask or fin, before veering off with remarkable agility. Older bulls rarely display their acrobatics for divers. They seem content to cruise by slowly, using their impressive bulk to intimidate. Sea lions have been known to steal fish from the stringers of spearfishing divers. They can be quite aggressive in this endeavor, so be forewarned.

## Harbor Seals

Divers frequently encounter harbor seals sticking their heads out of the water or observing other divers when diving in Monterey, as well as on the north coast. Mature males weigh 250 to 300lbs (114 to 136kg) and are approximately 5 to 6ft (1.5 to 1.8m) long. Harbor seals are distinguished easily from sea lions: seals are much smaller and stockier than sea lions, have no external ear flaps, have short front flippers, and their rear flippers cannot be turned forward. When startled or when moving away, seals always submerge by dropping backward into the water. (Sea lions will lunge forward with a porpoiselike motion.) If you watch seals move on land, they use an awkward, inchwormlike motion. (Sea lions, on the other hand, use their front and rear flippers to waddle.)

There are many dive sites in Monterey, including Otter Cove, McAbee Beach and Point Lobos, where young seals will initiate contact with divers. It is not unusual for them to mouth fins and gauges, grab onto legs, arms and tanks with their front flippers or peek over a diver's shoulder with apparent curiosity. Harbor seals feed on squid, octopuses, shellfish and many types of fish. They normally present a danger only to divers who are spearfishing.

Inquisitive harbor seals often become a second buddy during the dive.

# Shore Diving

The majority of the diving in Central and Northern California is shore diving, so you should be aware of the accepted safety techniques for entering and exiting the water. Although there are some minor differences in the skills taught in certification courses, it is generally held that, except on extremely calm days, divers should back into the surf with their fins on and their regulators in their mouths. In heavy surf, exit the water by crawling on all fours through the surf line, with your regulator in your mouth. It is also recommended that you reserve between 500 and 1,000psi in your tank for your exit, and select an alternate exit point in case the surf becomes dangerously rough at your preferred exit point during the course of the dive. Only when the ocean is calm and access is via a flat sandy beach should divers walk into the ocean and don their fins in waist-deep water.

Entering along the north coast, where there are few sandy beaches, can be even trickier. You must learn to enter the water over slippery, kelp-covered rocks or from rock ledges above the water level. Divers need to learn to time the height of the swells—it is easier to enter or exit the ocean as the swell rises. Be aware of rip currents and coastal currents, and be prepared to abort a dive when the conditions are hazardous. If you are a novice diver or are unfamiliar with the area, it is better to buddy up with an experienced diver who is familiar with the sites you want to dive.

When shore diving requires a long swim, it is a good idea for each diver to take a float. Several flotation devices are currently available. Though inflatable surf mats have gone the way of the Edsel, inner tubes and kickboards are easy-to-use alternatives.

# Boat Diving

Diving from a boat, whether it is a hired dive charter or a personal inflatable or kayak, allows divers to access sites that are offshore of otherwise inaccessible

Inflatables offer a stable platform for diving offshore reefs.

## Boat-Diving Safety Tips

Keep in mind a few safety rules about diving from inflatables, small hard-hull boats, dive boards and kayaks. Many divers anchor their boat and leave the vessel unattended. Be sure to check the anchor at the beginning of the dive to make sure it is firmly set on the bottom. It can be quite an inconvenience if you surface and find no boat in sight. Also, because ocean swells can quickly increase in size, let out at least 50% more anchor line than the depth where you are anchored. For example, if the water is 50ft (15m) deep, let out at least 75ft (23m) of rope. Dive boards and kayaks can be tied off to kelp beds. Dive flags are a must to make small boats more visible and to let boaters know that there are divers in the area. It is also a good idea to begin the dive by swimming up-current. At the end of the dive, ascend with at least 500psi so that if the kelp is thick at the surface, you can locate the boat, descend and swim back to it underwater.

coastal points or that are too far from shore to swim to. There are several dive charters now operating out of Monterey Harbor, together with a veritable fleet of inflatables and smaller hard-hull boats. The north coast currently has only one licensed dive charter operation, located at Albion Cove in Mendocino County. See the Listings section for dive boat operator details.

Inflatables are a popular way for independent divers to reach many dive sites, and with good reason. They are stable, relatively inexpensive, require little maintenance, are easy to maneuver and double as an excellent dive platform. Many hard-hull boats such as Boston Whalers and Makos have also become quite popular as dive boats and are able to make longer trips to some of the more remote sites.

Dive boards and kayaks also have become popular because of their versatility. They can be launched from tiny beach entries, are relatively inexpensive and greatly extend a shore diver's range.

The number of boat launch facilities available on the Monterey Peninsula is limited. There are two double ramps inside the Monterey Breakwater, a facility at Stillwater Cove (Pebble Beach), and a small ramp at Point Lobos (which can be used only for diving inside the reserve). Divers can launch inflatables at Limekiln Campground on the Big Sur coast. It is also possible to launch inflatables equipped with sand wheels across several of the sites that have flat sand beaches. On the north coast, a number of sites can accommodate small inflatables and kayaks. A few places permit launching medium and large inflatables and small hard-hull boats, such as at Timber Cove in Sonoma County, and Albion River and Noyo Harbor in Mendocino County.

# Certification Classes

Open Water classes are regularly conducted year-round by dive stores all over California. Open Water certification usually includes four classroom sessions, four pool sessions and four ocean dives. Some classes include an optional free-dive. The length and coverage of the classes vary slightly between instructors, certifying agencies and dive stores. Dive classes in Central and Northern California differ from certification classes in warm-water locales in that they teach students how to deal with kelp and how to enter and exit the water from sandy beaches and rocky shorelines.

Many beach sites in Monterey and on the north coast are commonly used for classes. These are usually sites that afford a little more protection and offer calmer conditions than most beach dives. In Monterey, the Breakwater, McAbee Beach, "inner" Lovers Point and Coral Street Beach are the most popular sites for novice classes. In Sonoma County, many ocean sessions are conducted at Stillwater Cove and Gerstle Cove. Van Damme is certainly the most protected and most popular site for classes in Mendocino County.

## Dive Site Icons

The symbols at the beginning of each dive site description provide a quick summary of some of the important characteristics of each site:

 Good snorkeling or free-diving site.

 Remains or partial remains of a wreck can be seen at this site.

 Sheer wall or drop-off.

 Deep dive. Features of this dive are found in water deeper than 90ft (27m).

 Strong currents may be encountered at this site.

 Strong surge (the horizontal movement of water caused by waves) may be encountered at this site.

 Shore dive. This site can be accessed from shore.

 Caves or caverns are a prominent feature of this site. Only experienced cave divers should explore inner cave areas.

 Marine preserve. Special protective regulations apply in this area.

# Pisces Rating System for Dives & Divers

The dive sites in this book are rated according to the following diver skill-level rating system. These are not absolute ratings but apply to divers at a particular time, diving at a particular place. For instance, someone unfamiliar with prevailing conditions might be considered a novice diver at one dive area, but an intermediate diver at another, more familiar location.

**Novice:** A novice diver should be accompanied by an instructor, divemaster or advanced diver on all dives. A novice diver generally fits the following profile:
◆ basic scuba certification from an internationally recognized certifying agency
◆ dives infrequently (less than one trip a year)
◆ logged fewer than 25 total dives
◆ little or no experience diving in similar waters and conditions
◆ dives no deeper than 60ft (18m)

**Intermediate:** An intermediate diver generally fits the following profile:
◆ may have participated in some form of continuing diver education
◆ logged between 25 and 100 dives
◆ dives no deeper than 130ft (40m)
◆ has been diving in similar waters and conditions within the last six months

**Advanced:** An advanced diver generally fits the following profile:
◆ advanced certification
◆ has been diving for more than two years and logged over 100 dives
◆ has been diving in similar waters and conditions within the last six months

Regardless of your skill level, you should be in good physical condition and know your limitations. If you are uncertain of your own level of expertise for a particular site, ask the advice of a local dive instructor. He or she is best qualified to assess your abilities based on the site's prevailing dive conditions. Ultimately, however, you must decide if you are capable of making a particular dive, a decision that should take into account your level of training, recent experience and physical condition, as well as the conditions at the site. Remember that conditions can change at any time, even during a dive.

Monterey attracts thousands of tourists each year to its internationally renowned aquarium, its quaint Fisherman's Wharf and its scenic shores. But Monterey's charm doesn't end at the water's edge. As California's premier dive destination, Monterey offers easy access to beach dives and offshore pinnacles that draw divers from all over Northern and Central California and beyond. The underwater spectacles include magnificent kelp forests, plentiful fish life, tapestries of colorful invertebrates and a variety of fascinating and inquisitive marine mammals.

A cruise through a kelp bed on a sunny day is akin to flying through a giant redwood forest. Although the sardines that spawned Cannery Row are no longer present in great numbers, the diversity and abundance of marine life that remains in the area is unmatched anywhere.

Sea otters, once hunted almost to extinction along the California coast, have staged a comeback and are now seen throughout the kelp beds along the shoreline of Monterey Bay. Sea lions, harbor seals, brown pelicans and other diving birds have a distinct presence along the coast, providing entertainment for tourists and divers alike. Divers frequently have close encounters with adolescent

Small octopuses change their shape and color to blend in with the reef.

seal pups that literally demand attention. Young sea lions often confront divers with "in your face" displays of playful aggressiveness, blowing bubbles and nipping at fins.

Dive sites inside Monterey Bay are generally protected from the prevailing northwest swells. Most dive locations are fairly shallow, with depths ranging from 20 to 70ft (6 to 21m), though there are a few exceptions. Visibility rarely exceeds 30ft (9m), and the best visibility occurs during the fall and

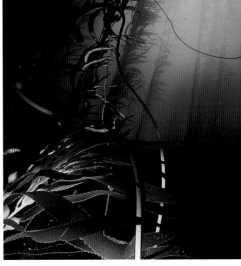

Kelp is important to the aquatic ecosystem.

## Deep & Wide

The Monterey Canyon, which lies offshore in the heart of the Monterey Bay National Marine Sanctuary, is so deep and wide that it rivals Arizona's Grand Canyon. The canyon drops to extreme depths, more than 10,000ft (3,000m) in the open ocean. In some places, such as Moss Landing and Monastery Beach, the canyon comes within a couple hundred yards of shore. When offshore winds and ocean currents cause upwellings, the nutrient-rich deep-ocean waters bring an incredible assortment of marine life into the shallows. These animals include magnificent jellyfish and long chains of transparent salps.

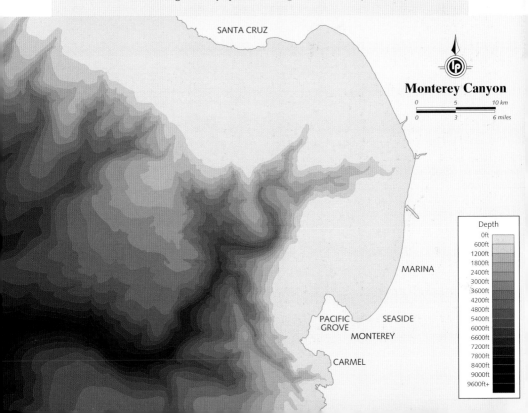

Colorful invertebrate tapestries attract divers to Monterey Bay.

early winter, when there's the least amount of plankton. Water temperatures usually range from 51 to 56°F (11 to 13°C).

Admittedly, the diving in this area is a bit more strenuous and fatiguing than warm-water destinations. Dealing with surf entries on beach dives, and with the surge and kelp, requires additional training. The chilly waters also demand more equipment, heavier weight belts and exposure suits that offer greater warmth.

## Monterey Bay Dive Sites

| | Good Snorkeling | Novice | Intermediate | Advanced |
|---|:---:|:---:|:---:|:---:|
| 1 Del Monte Beach | ● | | ● | |
| 2 Wharf #2 | | | ● | |
| 3 The Breakwater | ● | ● | | |
| 4 Metridium Field | | | ● | |
| 5 McAbee Beach | | ● | | |
| 6 Hopkins Reef | | ● | | |
| 7 Lovers Point Cove | ● | | ● | |
| 8 Otter Cove | ● | | ● | |
| 9 Inner Chase Reef | | | ● | |
| 10 Coral Street Beach | ● | ● | | |
| 11 Outer Chase Reef | | | ● | |
| 12 Sewers | | | | ● |
| 13 Point Pinos | ● | | | ● |

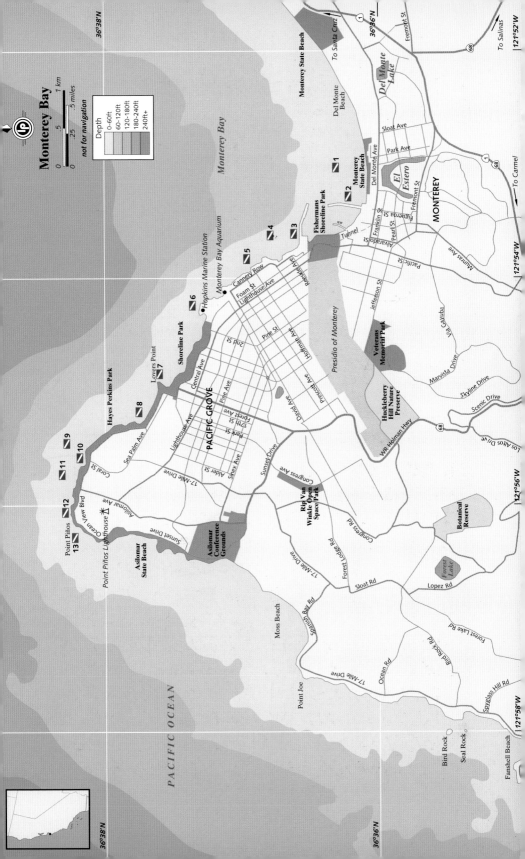

# 1 Del Monte Beach

Del Monte Beach is a long stretch of white sand that dominates the center of Monterey Bay. Though this area often experiences low visibility and heavy surf and surge, it is inhabited by several varieties of fish and plants that make it well worth a visit.

One of the most popular access points along Del Monte Beach is a spot called **The Laundromat**, named after the laundromat at the intersection of Park and Del Monte Avenues. The completely submerged remains of an old pier running perpendicular to the beach lie about 200 yards west of the end of Park Avenue.

Halibut follow this artificial reef into the shallow waters, feeding on crustaceans in the sand. These fish have flat, elongated bodies and are usually found lying partially buried in the sand or mud in 20ft to waist-deep water. Halibut are very timid, so the appearance of a diver usually causes these fish to dart off suddenly, creating a virtual sandstorm. But often they return to the same spot, or swim only a short distance before settling back into the sand.

**Location:** Intersection of Del Monte and Park Aves., Monterey

**Depth Range:** 10-60ft (3-18m)

**Access:** Shore

**Expertise Rating:** Intermediate

The relatively flat bottom is composed mostly of sand. A series of low shale ledges (or shoals) run parallel to the shore approximately 150 to 200 yards from the beach, extending from the Monterey Beach Hotel to approximately 200 yards north of Wharf #2. These ledges, in depths between 40 and 50ft, are often referred to as **Tanker Reef** or the

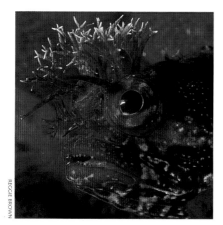

Fringe-head blennies are the "worst dressed."

Diving in kelp is like flying between redwoods.

**Shale Beds.** You can find the ledges easily throughout most of the year by looking for the narrow kelp bed that reaches from the ledges to the surface. In this area you will find a variety of marine life, including flounders, octopuses, fringe-head blennies, sponges and anemones. Divers often encounter many types of rays and skates parked on the ocean bottom. Closer to shore, in less than 20ft of water, fields of purple sand dollars pop out of the sand.

Another entry point used by divers is often referred to as **McDonald's**, near the McDonald's restaurant on Del Monte Avenue. This site is also near the Monterey Bay Kayak entry point. There is a fee parking lot at the nearby intersection of Del Monte Avenue and Camino El Estero. From this entry point you can reach the wreck of a "buffalo half track" amphibious personnel carrier, which lies at 20ft on an eelgrass bed found several hundred yards offshore. The shell of the wreck is covered with a variety of invertebrates including anemones, scallops and encrusting sponges.

# 2  Wharf #2

Wharf #2 is an excellent dive for macro-photography. To get to the site, turn onto Figueroa Street from Del Monte Avenue and park in the metered parking lot at the foot of the wharf. Divers must check in with the harbormaster to get permission to dive this site. The harbormaster's office is next to the boat launch ramps between Wharves #1 and #2. For safety reasons, divers are required to have a spotter either in a boat or on the wharf.

Enter from the flat sand beach just to the right of Wharf #2. Swim out along the concrete wharf until you reach the maze of wooden posts or pilings. The 30 to 40ft-high pilings provide a treasure trove of interesting and colorful marine life. Carpets of pink, lavender and orange corynactis (strawberry anemones) cover many of the pilings. Amid the anemones, large acorn barnacles reach for food with their pitchfork-shaped feet and suck plankton off their ornate plumage. Other pilings are covered with snow-white anemones, feather duster worms and reddish-brown bry-

**Location:** Intersection of Del Monte Ave. and Figueroa St., Monterey

**Depth Range:** 25-30ft (7.6-9.1m)

**Access:** Shore

**Expertise Rating:** Intermediate

ozoans. A wide variety of gaudy nudibranchs also populate this area.

Delicate feather duster worms adorn the pilings of Wharf #2.

Although this is probably the calmest site in Monterey and is not deeper than 30ft, it is not for novice divers. The base of the wooden columns is a virtual junkyard, replete with old shoes, tires, bottles and cans, and myriad other human castoffs. Because this area was and is used extensively by fishermen, there is also a great deal of monofilament fishing line, as well as hooks and even pieces of old gill nets. As a safety precaution, it is a good idea to carry a dive knife with a serrated edge, in case you have to cut yourself free of fishing line. Also, divers should keep their distance from anyone fishing from the wharf.

## 3    The Breakwater

On the northwest side of Monterey Harbor, a man-made rock jetty or breakwater extends 200 yards from the end of the Coast Guard pier. The Breakwater provides an excellent introduction to the topography and marine life you'll find throughout the Monterey Peninsula. Divers of all skill levels will find something of interest. This is one of the safest entry points in Monterey and is used frequently by diving instructors for checkout dives. The surf here is usually

**Location:** Intersection of Cannery Row and Foam St., Monterey

**Depth Range:** 20-60ft (6.1-18m)

**Access:** Shore or boat

**Expertise Rating:** Novice

calm (allowing for easy entries and exits), therefore there is normally little, if any, surge. Most trainees and novice divers stay fairly close to shore, in depths between 15 and 30ft.

You can access the site from the narrow, rocky beach at the foot of the stairs on the ocean side and just to the left (north) of the breakwater parking lot. Amenities near the intersection of Cannery Row and Foam Street include a grassy park, picnic benches, freshwater shower, a parking lot with a limited number of metered spaces, and a fee lot. On weekends from March through October, it is a good idea to arrive early to get a parking

Sea lions frequently perform an underwater ballet for divers at the Breakwater.

space. There is another access point at the foot of Reeside Avenue one block away. You'll find a double boat ramp on the inside of the breakwater between the restrooms and the Aquarius II dive store, and another boat ramp next to the harbormaster's office between Wharves #1 and #2.

You'll find some of the best diving along the northern (ocean) side of the rock jetty, where a kelp bed grows along the entire length of the breakwater. This is a good place to get a feel for kelp diving without having to worry about rough surf or strong surge. Enter the water from the beach at the bottom of the stairs and swim on the surface to the point where the jetty bends slightly to the right before descending.

The rock jetty slopes to a sandy bottom at 50 to 60ft that is home to a splendid array of filter feeders, including tube anemones and sea pens, protruding from the sand. Lavender and reddish-brown rainbow nudibranchs, which grow to more than 8 inches long, feed on the tentacles of these anemones. To locate the nudibranchs, look for white egg masses on the sides of the tubes. Though the visibility at the Breakwater is not usually as good as other parts of the Monterey Peninsula, the area has become popular with underwater photographers because of the excellent diversity of marine invertebrates.

Playful sea lions, sea otters, diving birds, octopuses and monkeyface eels also inhabit the area. If you swim all the way to the end of the jetty, you'll often find as many as 40 young sea lions waiting for a playmate! The sea lions disappear during late spring and early summer, when they make their annual trek to nearby rookeries.

The easy access and rock jetty also provide good reference points underwater, making it an excellent site for night dives. At night you may see octopuses out foraging on the sand, rays feeding on shellfish on the sand flats, hermit crabs and other crustaceans walking about and many sea pens protruding from the bottom.

Rainbow nudibranchs feed on tube anemones' tentacles.

## Sea Lion Pride

Animal behavior in the wild is fascinating and unpredictable. Though seals, otters and sea lions (the most common mammals that divers will encounter off the California coast) are generally friendly, they can become aggressive. Author Steve Rosenberg gives a first-person account of an unusual encounter with a sea lion.

"A group of sea lions can often be found hanging out at the surface near the end of the Coast Guard breakwater. One day I snorkeled out with a buddy and came across such a group of sea lions that appeared to be drifting aimlessly. Some were dozing and others were nipping playfully at each other. I dove down and surfaced in the middle of them to get some photos. They immediately exploded in a burst of activity, leaping out of the water and careening in every direction at once. This is typical young sea lion behavior.

"One young male lunged forward in a typical aggressive display, snapped its teeth within inches of my mask and then veered away. (I kept shooting photos.) He immediately turned around and peered intently at me as if to determine whether he had caused a reaction of any kind. He seemed disappointed and lunged for me again, this time blowing bubbles in my face before veering away. Again he stopped to assess the effectiveness of his tactics. (I kept shooting.) He kept up this behavior for about fifteen minutes until I ran out of film and he finally ran out of interest or patience.

"I have seen this type of aggressive behavior on many occasions over the years, but I have never seen one animal so intent upon getting a reaction and so disappointed by my amusement."

## 4 Metridium Field

Metridium Field lies in about 50 to 70ft of water. It got its name from the billowy white metridium anemones whose stalks reach up to 2ft in length and which cover the rocky outcroppings. It is about 200 yards offshore, where an imaginary line drawn from the tip of the breakwater to Point Cabrillo (Hopkins Marine Station) and a line drawn as an extension of Reeside Avenue would intersect.

You can swim to the area, but it's a fairly long journey (about 150 to 200

**Location:** Intersection of Cannery Row and Reeside Ave., Monterey

**Depth Range:** 50-70ft (15-21m)

**Access:** Shore or boat

**Expertise Rating:** Intermediate

yards to get to the near edge of the dive site). Swim straight out on a line from

Reeside Avenue. When you get to the outer edge of the kelp bed, continue swimming on the surface until you get to the imaginary line between Point Cabrillo and the end of the breakwater, being careful to avoid boat traffic.

Because of the heavy boat traffic in this area, it's safer to dive from a boat. Anchor at the location given above and follow the anchor line to the bottom— approximately 60ft down. Always check your anchor at the beginning of the dive to make sure it is securely set. It is also important to leave sufficient "scope" or slack in the anchor line to prevent sudden swells from yanking the anchor off the bottom.

When you descend, swim toward the northwest to find the greatest concentration of anemones. Small octopuses and crabs forage among the tube anemones and sea pens that dot the sandy bottom. Divers here frequently see bat rays, juvenile wolf eels, ocean sunfish (in the fall months), and an occasional bull sea lion cruising the outcroppings. When visibility is good, it is possible to hover 20 to 30ft from the bottom and scan literally acres of white anemones. Most of the time, though, visibility rarely exceeds 15 to 25ft because of the high concentration of plankton.

On sunny days when the visibility is good, Metridium Field is an excellent place for wide-angle photography. Get low and shoot upward to photograph the

metridiums against a green or black background. Be careful not to stir up sediment from the bottom, and sidelight with your flash to reduce backscatter.

If you swim in from Metridium Field you may encounter a large cannery pipeline (about 12 inches in diameter) half buried in the sand and rocks on the bottom. You can follow the pipeline back to the shallows at the foot of Reeside Avenue, or use your compass to return to the beach underwater. Of course, you can swim on the surface, but the kelp canopy is usually quite thick, making the surface swim slow and difficult.

An octopus hovers above billowy white metridium anemones.

## 5 McAbee Beach

This is another popular spot where scuba classes do their checkout dives. The entrance to the beach is at the intersection of Cannery Row and Hoffman Avenue, over a currently vacant lot between Spindrift Inn and El Torrito Restaurant, though future development may affect access. There is a convenient freshwater shower nearby, on the rear wall (facing the beach) of the Spindrift Inn.

**Location:** Intersection of Cannery Row and Hoffman Ave., Monterey

**Depth Range:** 25-35ft (7.6-11m)

**Access:** Shore

**Expertise Rating:** Novice

Divers must either gear up in the multilevel parking lot a block away from Cannery Row at the intersection of Hoffman Avenue and Wave Street and then walk to the beach, or drop their gear off at the beach and then park elsewhere. (Be aware of restrictions on the loading and unloading of dive gear, clearly posted along Cannery Row.) The multilevel parking lot is a fee lot and has no restroom facilities. On weekends, you need to arrive early to get a parking space, as visitors to Monterey's aquarium quickly take up most of the parking.

SHANNON ROSENBERG

Divers practice a crawling exit at McAbee Beach.

Curious harbor seal pups may approach divers at McAbee Beach.

Most people enter the water from the beach behind the hotel, though you can also enter below the radio tower, which you'll find to the left or north of the hotel. The rock-free beach slopes gently and the surf is usually light, making the entry safe and easy. A thick kelp forest extends from about 40 to 200 yards offshore. Swim straight out from the beach for 50 to 75 yards before descending to 25ft. The bottom, which consists of rock shelves and sandy patches, slopes gently to a maximum depth of 35ft at the outer edge of the kelp bed.

This jumbled rocky reef is inhabited by a multitude of marine denizens, including sea hares, crabs, chitons, anemones and rockfish. Decaying pipelines, once used by the canneries that thrived along Cannery Row, crisscross the area. These pipelines now serve as an artificial reef, attracting rockfish and a myriad of invertebrates.

The better diving is at the outer edge of the kelp bed, where some heavily encrusted pinnacles reach up from the sandy bottom. Take a compass reading to navigate under the kelp canopy, allowing you to make the trip out and then back to the beach with a minimum of effort.

## Kelp Harvesting

Kelp is one of the basic links in the food chain along the California coast, providing nutrients for a variety of mollusks and invertebrates, and shelter to a number of species. It is commercially harvested for use in agriculture, aquaculture and some food products. Divers will occasionally see kelp-harvesting machines while diving in the Monterey Bay National Marine Sanctuary. A controversy has arisen regarding the enforcement of kelp-harvesting regulations within the sanctuary, as well as the effects of harvesting on the kelp canopy and its web of interdependent species.

A report presented in September 1997 by the Coastal Solutions Group for NOAA (the National Oceanic and Atmospheric Administration) and the city of Monterey suggested that kelp harvesting had little detrimental effect on invertebrates that lived on the harvested kelp, such as snails, bryozoans and hydroids. The report implied that all such animals merely fell, re-attached to other kelp plants and went on with the business of growth and reproduction. The credibility of this report has been thrown into question, in that the same research group concurrently published a study of "Diver Disturbance In Kelp Forests" claiming it was a significant disturbance for divers, during the course of a dive, to accidentally knock a few snails from giant kelp blades by kicking their fins.

## 6 Hopkins Reef

Hopkins Reef, located between the buoys offshore from the Monterey Bay Aquarium and Point Cabrillo, is a protected marine reserve under study by marine biologists from Stanford University's Hopkins Marine Station. In the past, researchers have studied population densities and growth rates of invertebrates. The reef is accessible by boat or dive board only, and the ban against spearfishing is strictly enforced. Dive boats should anchor outside the research area (which is clearly marked with buoys) to avoid doing any damage to the bottom. Divers should be careful to stay off the bottom within the preserve to avoid disturbing any research projects in progress.

A thick kelp bed marks the shallow areas (20 to 45ft). Sea otters are frequently seen here floating on the surface or foraging for food. The bottom is made up of large granite formations with patches of sand between them. Kelp clings to the rocks, as do nudibranchs, sea hares, sea stars, anemones and crabs. The reef is also home to a variety of rock-

**Location:** Between Point Cabrillo and Monterey Bay Aquarium buoys

**Depth Range:** 30-60ft (9.1-18m)

**Access:** Boat or dive board

**Expertise Rating:** Novice

fish. As you work your way toward the outer edge of the kelp, the bottom drops away in terraces to fairly deep water. The outer reserve boundary, marked by the buoys, is in 60ft of water. This deeper area is best left to advanced divers. Be aware of the light to medium surge that is common at this site.

A sculpin makes a meal of an unwary shrimp.

Strawberry anemones decorate the area.

## Kelp Diving

While the rich marine life of the kelp forest is enjoyed by many experienced kelp divers, those who have never had the pleasure of diving in California's kelp beds may be a bit nervous at first. Once you learn the basics of kelp diving, you'll quickly find that there's little to fear. In fact, kelp can be an aid to divers. These long strands of sea-weed can show you which way the current is flowing. In areas where there is a lot of boat traffic, kelp can indicate safe areas in which to sur-face. Kelp beds are also a good area to tie off small boats, rafts and dive floats. But perhaps the best incen-tive to try kelp diving is the spectacular selection and abundance of marine life that lives within the kelp beds.

Of course, kelp can be hazardous if you get caught in it and panic. Whether free-diving or scuba diving, remember to follow a few simple precautions:

**Stay Alert** Be particularly aware of kelp at the surface where it can become so thick

Diving under the kelp canopy is easy if you follow a few simple precautions.

that you can't swim through it. Try to stay away from areas where kelp is extremely thick and always be aware of the surface canopy of kelp while ascending.

**Look for an Opening** As you ascend, always look up to locate an open space in the kelp canopy. Ascend with a reserve of air so that you can descend, if necessary, to find a clear opening through which to surface. Never try to fight through a layer of kelp to get to the surface.

**Save Enough Air to Return Underwater** It is much easier, less tiring and safer to swim beneath the kelp canopy than to do the "kelp crawl" over it.

**Don't Panic** During summer and early fall (when the kelp beds literally clog many of the coves) it is easy to get tangled in kelp, especially bull kelp, whose slender stalks grow close together. If you do become entangled in kelp, wait calmly for your dive buddy to help remove the problem strands. Kelp is very elastic and doesn't break easily when pulled, but will snap in two when bent over on itself.

## 7 Lovers Point Cove

Lovers Point is one of Pacific Grove's scenic tourist attractions, located on Ocean View Boulevard at the end of 17th Street. The parklike area is home to side-by-side coves on the inside (right side) of the point. The main cove is inside both the concrete breakwater and the point, and thus is the more protected of the two. In addition, the cove has a gently sloping sandy beach. This small area of sandy beach attracts swimmers, sunbathers, snorkelers, surfers, and families with young children, all of whom compete for a share of the limited space. In addition to these sightseers, the area is popular among divers, dive instructors and underwater photographers.

From Friday through Monday during April through September, city regulations limit divers' access via the east cove beach to mornings before 11:30am. There is unlimited access during other times of

**Location:** Intersection of Ocean View Blvd. and 17th St., Pacific Grove

**Depth Range:** 20-40ft (6.1-12m)

**Access:** Shore or boat

**Expertise Rating:** Intermediate

the week and year. No scuba gear is supposed to be left unattended on this beach at any time. The city is occasionally lenient about enforcing these regulations, so don't abuse the privilege of diving from here. Be courteous to others using this beach area!

The smaller cove lies between the concrete breakwater and the point. The surf often picks up here, attracting surfers. Entry from the west side of the point can be hazardous when the bay is rough.

The inside cove at Lovers Point offers one of the calmest beach entries in the Monterey area.

From these entry points, swim straight out and to the left about 100 yards to get to the better dive areas, at 30 to 40ft deep, with 10 to 20ft pinnacles on a sandy bottom. From the main cove it is a longer swim out—at least 75 yards until you get to a kelp bed in 20ft of water.

Visibility is generally good (from 30 up to 60ft). You'll find the best diving straight out from the western, ocean side of the point. The marine life is colorful and varied. Divers often encounter bat rays, torpedo rays, rockfish schools and harbor seals that cruise the sandy areas between the tall rocky outcroppings. The rocky surface is covered with a carpet of sponges, anemones, sea stars, barnacles and nudibranchs. Spearfishing is strictly prohibited at Lovers Point.

The area just off the point is relatively shallow (15 to 20ft) and the bottom consists mostly of large boulders and rocks—a popular spot for monkeyface eels. Monkeyface eels are not true eels and do not have large teeth. Some divers coax these somewhat shy fish from the caves with scraps of food and have managed to get monkeyface eels to eat right out of their hands. With the aid of a dive buddy to feed the fish, underwater photographers can come away with some unusual shots.

The only restrooms are in the park close to Ocean View Boulevard about midway between the two coves. There is limited parking along Ocean View Boulevard and the two-hour limit is strictly enforced.

Monkeyface eels are members of the prickleback family, related to blennies.

## 8 Otter Cove

Otter Cove is just a few blocks west of Lovers Point at the corner of Ocean View Boulevard and Sea Palm Avenue. The cove is often referred to as "Stinky Beach" because of the malodorous piles of decaying broken kelp pushed ashore by storms and heavy swells.

The narrow rocky beach can be easily reached by a stone stairway found in the middle of the beach. Entries can be difficult here, especially during low tide, because the water is very shallow for a long distance from the beach. In the shallow areas, brown algae and thick eelgrass cover most of the rocks. Even

**Location:** Intersection of Ocean View Blvd. and Sea Palm Ave., Pacific Grove

**Depth Range:** 25-55ft (7.6-17m)

**Access:** Shore or boat

**Expertise Rating:** Intermediate

when the ocean is calm, divers can fall on the slippery surfaces and become entangled in the long eelgrass. If the surf is at all heavy, divers risk getting tangled in the kelp or being thrown against the jagged rocks.

When the water is calm, the long swim out is definitely worth the effort. Once beyond the surf line (150 yards from shore), the bottom drops fairly abruptly to 50ft. Nearby is a haul-out site for a large group of harbor seals, which often join divers for much of the dive. One young harbor seal has earned a reputation for being particularly friendly to divers. The seal, nicknamed "Bandit," is easily recognized by its unusual markings—it has a white body and black circles around its eyes that resemble a mask.

As you swim farther out, you will find large rocky pinnacles protruding from the sandy bottom, forming miniature mountains. Dense patches of small strawberry anemones, decorator crabs, cup corals, large tealia anemones, sea stars, plume worms and sea hares cling to the rocks. Purple-ringed top shells, one of Monterey's most beautiful mollusks, can be found on kelp fronds or in the beds of strawberry anemones. Photographers easily can spend an entire dive in an area that's no larger than a tabletop.

**Eric's Pinnacle**, one of the best boat dives inside Monterey Bay, is located at the outer edge of the kelp bed at Otter Cove. The base of the pinnacle sits on the bottom between 50 and 65ft, and rises to within 18ft of the surface. The pinnacle has an abundance of colorful invertebrates, including carpets of strawberry anemones, sponges, nudibranchs, crabs and barnacles. You'll usually find a large number of lingcod perched on ledges on the sides of the pinnacle.

The reef that extends into the bay a good distance from shore and the variety of the terrain throughout Otter Cove provide an interesting dive. Without a compass, though, it's easy to lose your sense of direction. If you're beach diving, surface with at least 1,000psi and determine your distance and direction from shore, then descend under the kelp again to make the return trip to the beach. The kelp can get fairly thick in this area, so it is usually easier and safer to return to shore by swimming under the kelp than by trying to crawl over it at the surface.

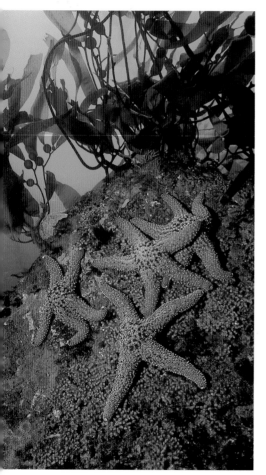

Giant sea stars are one of the rocky reef's key predators.

## Solitary but Not Alone

Orange cup coral (*Balanophyllia elegans*) is a species of solitary (or stony) coral that is frequently found on California's rocky reefs. Though individuals do not share a calcareous skeleton with others of the species, they will grow only a short distance apart. They tend to live in "family" groups: The larva generally move only a short distance from their "mother" before attaching and growing into new polyps. A full-grown individual is about 1 inch (2.5cm) in diameter when fully extended.

## 9 Inner Chase Reef

Inner Chase Reef lies north of Coral Street Beach, just inside the western tip of Monterey Bay. Vulnerable to the prevailing northwesterly swells, this site can be treacherous during rough weather but beautiful when the winds are calm. Because of its distance from shore (300 to 400 yards) most divers travel to Inner Chase Reef by boat. This is unfortunate, because the terrain on the way out is worth seeing. If you're an experienced diver and would like to try the swim (on calm days only), leave from the beach to the right, or west, of the natural breakwater and head out slightly to the left of the point. Take a surf mat, inner tube or other flotation device with you to give your legs a rest during the long trip back to the beach. Dive boards, which are easy to launch from Coral Street, also can help get you to the outer edge of the kelp bed.

Inner Chase Reef consists of a series of rocky ridges with numerous crevices and caves that run parallel to shore in 40 to 60ft of water. The reef is covered with large patches of corynactus (strawberry anemones), many types of tealia anemones, cobalt blue and orange puff-

**Location:** Intersection of Ocean View Blvd. and Coral St., Pacific Grove

**Depth Range:** 40-90ft (12-27m)

**Access:** Shore, boat or dive board

**Expertise Rating:** Intermediate

ball sponges, coralline algae and a variety of nudibranchs.

Just east of Inner Chase Reef is **Aumentos Reef**, another site that dive

Sheephead are now residents of Monterey, courtesy of El Niño.

operators visit when the sea is too rough or as a second site inside the bay. This area consists of massive granite blocks that rise to within 40ft of the surface. The reef is covered with encrusting invertebrates, strawberry and tealia anemones, and bright yellow zoanthid anemones. On the inshore side of the reef, the bottom drops to 55ft. On the outside, fluffy white metridium anemones cover the vertical walls. The walls terrace down to the rock and sand bottom at 80 to 90ft. The fish life includes schools of blue rockfish, sheephead, cabezon, lingcod and surfperch.

## 10  Coral Street Beach

Because the entry to Coral Street Beach is well protected, it is often used by instructors to teach novice divers, particularly when the ocean is calm. The beach is at the corner of Ocean View Boulevard and Coral Street, where a natural breakwater running south to north protects the beach area from prevailing northwest swells. The beach is a few feet below street level, separated from the sidewalk by a short rock wall. The steps are on the west (left) side of the beach closest to the breakwater. Parking is readily available on the street, but there are no restroom facilities.

**Location:** Intersection of Ocean View Blvd. and Coral St., Pacific Grove

**Depth Range:** 15-40ft (4.6-12m)

**Access:** Shore

**Expertise Rating:** Novice

Enter the water on the west end (left side) of the beach inside the breakwater, where you'll find a wide channel that drops quickly to about 20ft. The flat sandy bottom is littered with old abalone

Coral Street Beach is protected from swells by a natural breakwater.

shells. Rocky boulders covered with a thick coat of coralline algae sit along both sides of the channel.

As you swim north out of the cove, the bottom consists of miniature pinnacles and ridges, rising to within 15ft of the surface. Invertebrates commonly found in this area include Hopkin's rose and lemon nudibranchs, ringed top shells and encrusting sponges. In the summer months, divers will frequently find halibut lying motionless, half buried in the sand or perched on the rocky substrate. Harbor seals often poke their heads up to watch divers enter the water and occasionally make an appearance during a dive. This site is an excellent place for underwater photography because the unusually clear water allows plenty of light to penetrate to the bottom.

Coastal currents that run parallel to the shore can get quite strong beyond the breakwater on the west side of the cove. You might find it easier to swim underwater most of the way back to the beach rather than fight the surface currents. Once inside the end of the breakwater, the water is usually calm. The major drawback of Coral Street Beach is that the kelp gets very thick during the late summer and fall, reducing the amount of light and making it difficult to avoid getting tangled in the kelp stalks.

Look for halibut during the summer, when they come to shallow waters to reproduce.

## 11 Outer Chase Reef

Outer Chase Reef is often visited by commercial dive operators and by divers who launch their boats at one of the ramps in Monterey Bay. Because of its distance from shore (500 yards), it is accessible only by boat. The site, near Point Pinos, has a number of drop-offs, some of which fall to 100ft. A high archway lined with white metridium anemones sits at the edge of one of these drop-offs. Sponges, bryozoans and colonies of anemones

**Location:** North of Point Pinos

**Depth Range:** 40-100ft (12-30m)

**Access:** Boat

**Expertise Rating:** Intermediate

completely cover the walls. This is an excellent area for macrophotography, thanks to an incredible array of nudibranchs, sea stars and other creatures, which comb the bottom for food.

Be aware that the swells can get fairly large at Outer Chase Reef, especially in the afternoon. Set anchors securely, with plenty of slack left in the line. As always, begin your dive by swimming into the current and return with the current. If the ocean is rough, this site should be avoided because it lies directly in the teeth of the prevailing northwest swells.

Outer Chase Reef offers photogenic nudibranchs.

## 12 Sewers

The entry to Sewers is a rocky stretch of coastline just inside Monterey Bay, on the east side of Point Pinos. This site derives its name from the treatment plant across the road from the entry, but rest assured that this doesn't pose a threat to divers or water quality. There is an unpaved parking area parallel to Ocean View Boulevard west of the intersection of Asilomar Avenue.

Usually you'll find large swells, big waves and fairly strong currents—not ideal conditions for diving. You can get

**Location:** Near Ocean View Blvd. west of Asilomar Ave., Pacific Grove

**Depth Range:** 40-80ft (12-24m)

**Access:** Shore

**Expertise Rating:** Advanced

in the water at this site only on those rare days when the ocean is extremely calm. When there is a south swell or when the winds come from a southerly direction, the surf at Sewers can disappear completely. Though this is not a seasonal occurrence, it happens more often from late spring through early fall than at other times.

All of the entry points at Sewers require navigating through a maze of rocks. It is usually easier to enter the water as the tide is going out. At low tide it is too shallow to swim out, requiring that you walk carefully over the slippery rocks and put your fins on once you get into waist-deep water. It is best to dive here with someone familiar with the site.

Swim toward the kelp bed, which can normally be seen just offshore to the north and slightly east (to the right) of the entry points. The water is between 10 and 20ft deep on the inshore side of the kelp bed. Seagrass covers most of the nearshore rocks. The varied terrain consists of massive rocks, sand channels and mini canyons. As you move into deeper water, coralline algae, encrusting sponges, weedy kelp and palm kelp are prevalent. Beneath the dense kelp canopy lives a

wide variety of fish, including surfperch, cabezon, rockfish, painted greenlings and an occasional wolf eel. As you swim northward and away from shore, the bottom terraces downward in a series of ledges and holes.

Monterey boasts huge sunflower sea stars.

## 13  Point Pinos

Point Pinos is at the western tip of the point along the southern edge of Monterey Bay. The area is usually awash in white foam and spray from the waves pounding on the rocky shoreline. Dive this site only when the ocean is calm. Though this dive is normally done from a boat on very calm days, you can occasionally access it from the beach. The beach entry is adjacent to and west of the Sewers dive site and shares the same dirt parking area along the ocean side of Ocean View Boulevard. The closest cross street is Asilomar Avenue,

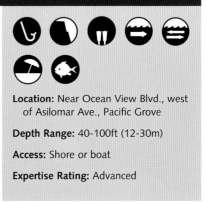

**Location:** Near Ocean View Blvd., west of Asilomar Ave., Pacific Grove

**Depth Range:** 40-100ft (12-30m)

**Access:** Shore or boat

**Expertise Rating:** Advanced

bordering the Pacific Grove municipal golf course.

On calm days, this can be a spectacular dive spot, especially in the late fall and early winter months when the visibility can reach 50 to 60ft. The kelp bed, which consists mostly of bull kelp and giant kelp, is usually sparse because of the heavy wave action in this area. The bottom terraces downward and is characterized by massive granite walls and boulders. A variety of invertebrates, including anemones, bryozoans, tunicates, rock scallops and sponges, thickly covers the rocky surfaces. Divers will frequently see bat rays, large lingcod and many of the rarer rockfish, such as rosy rockfish, tree rockfish and china rockfish. This is one of only a few sites in Monterey where there are red gorgonian sea fans, which divers can find clinging to the granite ledges at depths below 80ft. The sea fans make a striking subject for wide-angle photos.

White-spotted rose anemones are one of many beautiful anemones on the outer reefs.

Point Pinos is part of the Pacific Grove Marine Gardens Fish Refuge. It is legal to take finfish, and is popular with free-divers for spearfishing. It is illegal to take anything else, such as invertebrates.

Red gorgonians add a splash of color to California reefs as far north as the Monterey Peninsula.

Carmel is just a few miles south of Monterey and is part of the Monterey Peninsula. Most of the dive sites in Carmel Bay are more exposed to the weather than those in Monterey Bay, so the water is rougher, the surf higher and the surge stronger. Carmel does not attract as many divers as Monterey Bay because there are fewer beach access points and the main boat-launch facilities are miles away in Monterey Harbor.

Dive sites also tend to be deeper, with walls dropping well below sport-diving limits. The Carmel Trench (the submarine canyon in Carmel Bay) reaches to within 200 yards (185m) of the shore at the north end of Monastery Beach. The canyon drops off sharply, falling well below 1,000ft (300m) just 1 mile (1.6km) north of Point Lobos. Then, continuing to the northwest, the canyon plummets below 7,000ft (2,100m) just 6 miles (9.7km) away, where it meets the Monterey submarine canyon. During the spring and summer months, northwesterly winds drive the surface waters out to sea, allowing nutrient-rich waters to rise from the depths of the trench. These waters support an impressive community of plants and animals and occasionally bring a host of deepwater animals into the bay.

The proximity of the Carmel Trench keeps the water a few degrees cooler than Monterey Bay, with temperatures averaging 49 to 52°F (9 to 12°C) at the surface and dropping as low as 46°F (7°C) at depth. One significant benefit of the cold upwelling is that the water clarity can be substantially better in Carmel Bay than in Monterey Bay, with visibility often exceeding 60ft (18m) at the Pinnacles, Mono Lobo, Monastery Beach and Point Lobos. If you can withstand the cold, you're in for some spectacular dives.

Sea lions, common along the Monterey Peninsula, are often playfully aggressive with divers.

Point Joe
Moss Beach
121°58'W
121°56'W
To
Pacific Grove

Spanish Bay Rd
17-Mile Drive
Rip Van Winkle
Open Space Park
David Ave
Prescott Ave
Presidio of Mo

Forest Lodge Rd
Congress Rd
Forest Lodge Rd

17-Mile Drive
Sloat Rd
SFB Morse Drive
WR Holman Hwy
Huckleberry Hill
Nature Preserve
Veterans
Memorial Par
36
36°36'N
Ocean Rd

Bird Rock Rd
Lopez Rd
Forest
Lake
68
Marvista Drive
Via C

Bird Rock
Stevenson Drive
Botanical
Reserve
Sunridge Rd
Los Altos Drive
Scenic Drive
Skyline Drive

Seal Rock
Forest Lake Rd

Fanshell Beach
Spyglass Hill Rd
Monte
68
36°34'N

14
Cypress Point
Crocker
Grove

17-Mile Drive

Sunset Point
Cypress Drive
Palmero Way
PEBBLE BEACH
17-Mile Drive

36°34'N

Stillwater Cove
16
2nd Ave
Carpenter St

Pescadero
Point
Arrowhead
Point

15
Ocean Ave
CARMEL
8th Ave
San Carlos St
Junipero Ave

San Antonio Ave
Scenic Rd
Mission
Trails Park

Carmel Bay
Carmel Beach
City Park
13th Ave

PACIFIC OCEAN
17
Carmel Point
Bay View Ave
Ocean View Ave
Scenic Rd
Carmel River
Lagoon & Wetland
Nature Preserve
Carmel River
Rio R

18
Carmel River
State Beach
36°32'N
19
Ribera Rd
Cuesta Way
1

20
Carmel Bay

Point Lobos
21
Monastery
Beach
0      .5
0    .25    .5 mi

Bluefish
Cove
22
Whaler's
Cove
not for navigation

Point Lobos State Reserve
Depth
0-60ft
60-120ft
120-180ft
180-240ft
240ft+

To
Big Sur
121°58'W
121°56'W

## Carmel Bay Dive Sites

| | Good Snorkeling | Novice | Intermediate | Advanced |
|---|---|---|---|---|
| **14 Cypress Point** | | | ● | |
| **15 Ocean Pinnacles** | | | ● | |
| **16 Stillwater Cove** | | ● | | |
| **17 Copper Roof House** | ● | | | ● |
| **18 Carmel River Beach** | ● | | ● | |
| **19 Carmel Meadows** | ● | | | ● |
| **20 Monastery Beach** | | | | ● |
| **21 Mono Lobo Wall** | | | ● | |
| **22 Point Lobos State Reserve** | ● | ● | ● | |

# 14   Cypress Point

Cypress Point is usually considered the northernmost limit of Carmel Bay. Divers should not attempt to dive this site except on extremely calm days. Because this area is dived infrequently, the fish are abundant and easy to approach. They are generally indifferent to or even curious about the presence of divers.

When conditions are calm enough for you to get in the water, the north side of the point (outside of the wash rocks) is usually the safest area to dive. Visibility can be quite good—between 40 and 50ft. The bottom is a combination of granite pinnacles, huge boulders and sandy channels from 30 to 80ft deep. Most of the rocky surfaces are covered with a layer of coralline algae. There is usually a dense bed of bull and giant kelp, except when it has been torn away by heavy storms.

**Location:** Between Point Joe and Pescadero Point

**Depth Range:** 30-80ft (9.1-24m)

**Access:** Boat

**Expertise Rating:** Intermediate

Look for red gorgonians on deep walls.

As with any rocky area with a lot of water movement, there is a healthy assortment of invertebrates, including filter feeders such as tube worms, sponges and tunicates. There are also a few gorgonians in deeper areas, and you may find the somewhat rare California hydrocoral adding a splash of color to the rocky bottom. Large lingcod can frequently be found hiding in deep holes in the reef.

## 15 Ocean Pinnacles

This is one of Monterey Peninsula's premier dive destinations. Even if you plan to do only a few dives in the area, Ocean Pinnacles should be on your agenda. The only way to reach the pinnacles is by boat. Most dive charters operating out of Monterey visit here regularly, or you can make the 10-mile trip from the launch ramps inside Monterey Harbor. It is possible to launch at Pebble Beach (Stillwater Cove), but facilities are minimal (a boat hoist is available), parking needs to be

**Location:** West of Pescadero Point

**Depth Range:** 40-110ft (12-34m)

**Access:** Boat

**Expertise Rating:** Intermediate

prearranged, and usage rules are complicated at best. See Stillwater Cove dive site description for details.

Massive schools of blue rockfish, once common in Monterey, are occasionally encountered at the Pinnacles.

The pinnacles are actually two separate underwater mountains about a quarter mile apart. As a land reference point, look for a large pink house with a high tower, appropriately nicknamed "The Castle House," which lies north-northeast of the Pinnacles. Once you see the castle house, just look for the kelp bed offshore, or for the swell that pops up out of the water over the inner pinnacle. The inner pinnacle, which extends to within 12ft of the surface, is three-quarters of a mile offshore between Pescadero Point and Cypress Point. The top of the outer pinnacle (found west-southwest of the inner pinnacle) is actually a series of flat plateaus in 45 to 65ft of water. Each pinnacle is like a jagged mountain peak, with steep drop-offs and narrow canyons falling away to depths in excess of 100ft. Only advanced divers should explore these deeper regions.

The kelp's slender stalks reach up from reefs as far as 100ft below, forming a thick and imposing canopy at the surface. Massive schools of blue rockfish can be found hanging motionless just beneath the kelp canopy. One of the most incredible things about this reef area is that every square inch of the surface is blanketed with colorful invertebrates. From 60 to 90ft there are whole colonies of pink, purple and orange hydrocoral—a hydrozoan that is found on offshore reefs and pinnacles where the currents are strong, the water is clean and the plankton is abundant. Photographers will find this area to be a miniature wonderland of nudibranchs, shrimp, barnacles and tube worms.

## 16 Stillwater Cove

On days when heavy seas and strong winds cancel a trip to Ocean Pinnacles, charter boats often duck into Stillwater Cove. The substitution is good for photographers, because Stillwater Cove offers an excellent chance to work on photos of kelp and divers. The visibility is quite good and the uneven terrain adds drama to the many photo opportunities. But don't underestimate the sport-diving possibilities. Close to shore you can find species of fish that many divers think inhabit only Southern California waters, such as opaleye and sheephead.

When the northwest winds kick up, the cove turns into a glassy pond, lying protected behind the shelter of Pescadero Point. The area has a public beach entry where you can shore dive or launch small inflatables or dive boards year-round at no

**Location:** Inside (east of) Pescadero Point

**Depth Range:** 20-50ft (6.1-15m)

**Access:** Shore, boat, dive board or inflatable

**Expertise Rating:** Novice

Stillwater is a great place to work on photos of kelp and divers.

charge. Also, a renovated concrete pier is equipped with a hoist for launching boats. Currently, the boat-hoist facility operates between Memorial Day (late May) and Labor Day (early September). The hoist is taken down during other times of the year. The cost is $15. Check to see what additional equipment, if any, is required for launches. Six parking spaces are reserved for the public, but these are given away when other spaces are filled. If you get there after the lunch crowd arrives, you'll usually have trouble finding parking. Restroom facilities and a public telephone are also available. Contact the Pebble Beach Corporation (☎ 831-625-8520) for information about diving and parking reservations, entrance fees and boat launch fees and requirements.

## 17 Copper Roof House

Copper Roof House is named for the green copper roof of a nearby house designed by the famed American architect Frank Lloyd Wright. Wright built the house in the shape of a ship, a fitting testament to the brutal weather that sometimes afflicts the area. Only advanced divers should explore this site, which lies in the jaws of the northwest swells and can become quite treacherous even during the best conditions.

You can get to the beach access point via the stairway at the corner of Martin

**Location:** Intersection of Martin Way and Scenic Rd., Carmel

**Depth Range:** 20-60ft (6.1-18m)

**Access:** Shore or dive board

**Expertise Rating:** Advanced

Way and Scenic Road. The stairway is often damaged by winter storms and signs are usually posted when it is unsafe.

Giant sea hares are common in Carmel Bay.

When conditions permit diving, enter the water at the south end of the wide beach and swim toward the north end of the kelp bed that surrounds the point. You'll likely find schools of blue, olive and black rockfish at the edges of the kelp beds.

A reef at 50 to 60ft stretches in a jagged line from the point at Copper Roof to the wash rocks outside Stillwater Cove. Approximately 500 yards offshore the reef is broken by a number of sandy channels, a spot favored by halibut and several varieties of rockfish.

## 18 Carmel River Beach

Carmel River Beach is a large sandy area near the mouth of the Carmel River. When the ocean is flat, this area can be a great sightseeing or spearfishing spot. When there is a swell, this shallow area can be quite surge-prone, and the surf can make entry and diving conditions hazardous. Nevertheless, an interesting rocky reef, adequate parking and restroom facilities make this site popular with local divers. Enter Carmel River Beach at the corner of Scenic Road and Ocean View Avenue, about 1,000ft from the parking lot entrance. Many divers prefer the diving at the north end of the beach. There is less to see off the middle of the beach because the bottom is primarily sand with scattered rocky outcroppings.

Swim out around the rocky point to the right (north) and descend at the edge of the kelp bed. Inside the kelp bed, the bottom is between 20 and 30ft. Within the dense kelp forest you'll find lingcod, cabezon and a variety of rockfish and other colorful marine life. The bottom is rocky with large boulders covered by coralline algae. This is a good area to find a variety of nudibranchs.

Outside the kelp bed the bottom drops to 50ft, and pinnacles protrude from the sand bottom. Some of these minia-

**Location:** Intersection of Ocean View Ave. and Scenic Rd., Carmel

**Depth Range:** 20-60ft (6.1-18m)

**Access:** Shore

**Expertise Rating:** Intermediate

ture seamounts are 20ft high, creating mini walls to explore. These walls are covered with patches of strawberry anemones, plume worms and sponges. While most divers find the area satisfying, the visibility is rarely good enough for anything but close-up photography, and the selection of macrophotography subjects isn't as great here as at some other spots nearby.

Sea lemons are one of the largest and most commonly seen nudibranchs in California.

## 19 Carmel Meadows

The entry point to Carmel Meadows is close to the intersection of Ribera Road and Cuesta Way. To reach this area, turn west from Highway 1 onto Ribera Road, about a mile south of the foot of Ocean Avenue. There is parking for about six cars. A long stairway made of railroad ties leads down to the beach entry, which lies between Carmel River Beach (to the north) and Monastery Beach (to

**Location:** Near intersection of Ribera Rd. and Cuesta Way, Carmel

**Depth Range:** 30-40ft (9-12m)

**Access:** Shore

**Expertise Rating:** Advanced

Tube anemones move with the surge.

the south). Both ends of the beach are bordered by large rocky outcroppings. The best dive site is north of the rocky outcropping bordering Monastery Beach.

The bottom terraces into the Carmel Trench from the drop-off just a short swim offshore. There is a sandy area at 30 to 40ft where divers frequently find rainbow nudibranchs feeding on the tentacles of tube anemones, which are prevalent in this area. The rocky surfaces are covered with anemones and an assortment of other invertebrates such as barnacles, cup corals and nudibranchs.

## 20 Monastery Beach

Monastery Beach, located about 4 miles south of the intersection of Highway 1 and Highway 68, is one of the best-known dive sites on the Monterey Peninsula. You can enter the water at the kelp beds at either end of the beach. The surf tends to be rough in the center of the beach, and there is nothing but sandy bottom separating the kelp beds.

On most beaches, the swell rises gradually and breaks when it reaches a crest. At Monastery, the sea remains flat until it is close to the beach, then jumps up a short distance from shore and breaks abruptly. The surf is very unpredictable

**Location:** 4 miles (6.4km) south of Hwy 68, Carmel

**Depth Range:** 30-100ft (9.1-30m)

**Access:** Shore

**Expertise Rating:** Advanced

and can go from 1ft to more than 4ft in a matter of 30 minutes or less. This can make entries and exits extremely difficult except on very calm days. When the surf is moderate, divers should enter and exit with caution, but even experienced divers should avoid the area when the surf is heavy. No one should dive Monastery Beach without being properly trained in surf entries and exits.

If you enter from the north end of the beach, follow the edge of the kelp bed straight out. About 75 yards offshore, the bottom drops to about 30ft. This part of the site is outstanding for macrophotography despite the surge frequently encountered here. This area is full of colorful invertebrates of all kinds. Look for ringed top snails, lemon nudibranchs, large tealia anemones, sponges and kelp crabs.

The head of a deep submarine canyon climbs up into the bay just beyond the largest wash rock on the outer (western) edge of the kelp bed at the north end of Monastery Beach. There is a muddy, boulder-strewn slope or

A diver swims out to a kelp bed from south Monastery Beach.

wall at around 90ft, where you'll often find large lingcod. The bottom drops off sharply at this point, so exercise caution. It is popular for divers to follow this slope to depths exceeding 100ft, just to say they did. Keep track of your depth and the time—it's easy to lose track while watching the occasional bat ray, electric ray, leopard shark or blue shark winding its way through the kelp. Be sure to have a sufficient reserve of air in order to maneuver through the kelp and get through the surf on your return to shore.

The south end of Monastery Beach is more protected than the north end, making it possible to dive the site when conditions at the north end are too hazardous. The rocky bottom, which boasts excellent color and variety inside the kelp bed, doesn't drop below 60ft until you are several hundred yards offshore.

## Hydrocorals

California hydrocoral is not a true, reef-building coral but a colony of individual hydro-zoans. As they grow they develop a shared calcareous skeletal structure resembling stubby staghorn coral. The colonies grow very slowly, taking more than 20 years to reach a height of 10 to 12 inches (25 to 30cm). Divers may find pink, orange or purple hydrocoral on offshore reefs and pinnacles where strong currents provide the corals with an abundance of planktonic food. Though this beautiful coral was once commercially harvested, it is now illegal to collect hydrocoral in state waters.

## 21 Mono Lobo Wall

Mono Lobo Wall is at the edge of the kelp bed midway between the south end of Monastery Beach and Point Lobos State Reserve. Realistically, this site can be accessed only by charter boats, inflatables or other boats launched from Monterey Bay, although strong swimmers have been known to swim out from the south end of Monastery Beach. The Wall is not a good place to anchor when there is a heavy swell. There are a lot of wash rocks near shore both above and just under the surface. The large swells can easily push boats up against these rocks.

**Location:** South end of Carmel Bay

**Depth Range:** 40-100ft (12-30m)

**Access:** Boat or inflatable

**Expertise Rating:** Intermediate

When the ocean is smooth, this can be a spectacular dive spot. Morning, when the water is relatively calm, is usually the best time to dive. During the afternoon the wind and swells pick up. Because it faces into prevailing northwest swells, the area can become pretty rough.

The major attraction at Mono Lobo is a series of vertical granite walls that drop from 30ft to beyond 100ft. The walls are blanketed with colonies of tiny pink, lavender and orange anemones, orange and yellow feather duster tube worms, chestnut cowries, and sea stars of every size and shape imaginable. This is one of the few places in Northern or Central California where both pink and lavender hydrocorals can be found above 50ft. Within the kelp forests you'll find rays, giant sunfish, harbor seals and other large marine denizens wending their way through schools of blue rockfish.

## 22 Point Lobos State Reserve

Point Lobos State Reserve is about 4 miles south of Carmel on Highway 1. Because Point Lobos is a state park and a marine reserve, no plants or animals may be removed or disturbed in any way. In addition, the number of divers is restricted (and enforced) to maintain a balance between preserving the underwater park's natural state and protecting underwater recreational opportunities for the public. Only 15 buddy teams of two to three divers may dive here each day. Don't forget your C-card, as proof of dive certification is required.

**Location:** 4 miles (6.4km) south of Carmel

**Depth Range:** 20-110ft (6.1-33m)

**Access:** Shore or boat

**Expertise Rating:** Novice (Whaler's Cove), Intermediate (Bluefish and Coal Chute Coves)

Reservations, which can be made up to two months in advance, are recommended for weekday dives and are necessary for weekends and holidays. To

## Close Encounters

Author Steve Rosenberg reflects on a memorable dive at Point Lobos:

"I was diving with a friend in Point Lobos on a Friday morning in early summer. It was an unusually calm and bright sunny day. The dive had been enjoyable with superb 60ft visibility, but unspectacular. We were about to head in when I looked at my buddy and saw something quite surprising. The head of a young harbor seal was resting on his shoulder, as if trying to figure out what my friend was looking at.

"For the next 45 minutes the seal bounced back and forth between the two of us, bestowing hugs with its flippers, mouthing fins and hoses, never going more than a few feet away from us. From time to time, it would roll over on its back in front of one of us, literally demanding to have its tummy scratched. When we were low on air and began heading back to the ramp, the seal erupted in a flurry of activity, shooting up out of the water and rocketing back into us (actually bumping into us) as if expressing displeasure and frustration we were leaving."

make reservations call ☎ 831-624-8413 or visit the park's scuba webpage at pt-lobos.parks.state.ca.us/scuba/scuba .shtml. There is a $7 non-refundable reservation fee, as well as a $7 charge for each vehicle entering the park. Park hours are 9am to 7pm daily spring through fall and to 5pm in the winter.

Diving at Point Lobos is restricted to **Whaler's Cove** and **Bluefish Cove**. All dives must start at the boat ramp in Whaler's Cove; from here divers can swim out or launch small inflatable boats or kayaks. (You can't launch boats outside to dive within the park boundaries.) Facilities at Whaler's Cove include a parking lot, restrooms, picnic tables and freshwater rinsing hoses.

**Whaler's Cove** is covered with a thick layer of kelp most of the year, making swimming on the surface difficult at best. The sandy bottom inside the cove is littered with rocks and boulders. The maximum depth inside Whaler's Cove is

about 50ft, dropping to about 70ft just outside the cove mouth.

Directly across from the launch ramp you'll find tunnels and caves in **Coal Chute Cove**, a small cove at the northeast end of Whaler's Cove. To enter a large tunnel that goes through the southeastern edge of Coal Chute Cove, swim along the bottom on the right (south) side of the cove. The tunnel opening is at about 30ft.

Divers and snorkelers will find the shallows around the wash rocks to the left (west) side of Whaler's Cove mouth an excellent place to watch harbor seals sunbathing and sea otters foraging for food. It is not unusual for the younger harbor seals to interact with divers, doling out hugs and nibbling on fins.

To the left (west) of Whaler's Cove, a maze of huge rocks and canyons brimming with docile rockfish marks the area around Cannery Point. This point is also known as Bird Rock because it is covered with the white guano that marks the birds' perpetual presence.

Many local divers consider **Bluefish Cove** to be the best dive site in the reserve. Some parts of this cove are harder to access than others because the water is deeper, more exposed and frequently rougher than other areas inside the park. For these reasons, this area is most suitable for intermediate and advanced divers. Certainly, there's some spectacular scenery to explore.

On the east side of Bluefish Cove (next to Bird Rock), canyons, small pinnacles, crevices, large boulders and small caves shelter an assortment of rockfish, crabs and anemones. Along the west side of the cove, solitary pinnacles rise from the flat sandy bottom 100ft below the surface. In the open areas between the pinnacles you may encounter bat rays, sunfish, sea lions, schools of rockfish and an occasional blue shark. Along the outside of the cove, stretching from Bird Rock to the middle of the cove mouth, an incredible wall lies in waters ranging from 40ft to more than 100ft.

The reef areas of Bluefish Cove are a tapestry of color. It isn't uncommon to find 15 to 20 different types of nudibranchs on the outer walls during a single dive. Visibility here is generally better than other dive sites around the Monterey Peninsula, often exceeding 50ft.

Because marine life is protected within the boundaries of the park, most of the fish appear almost tame. In the fall, photographers can get superb close-up shots of the lingcod that come inshore to lay their eggs. Male lingcod and cabezon will stubbornly guard their egg nests against intruders, including scuba divers. Divers will often encounter leopard sharks in the flat sandy areas of the park, especially from November through April, when the sharks seek the quiet protection of the coves to give birth to their young. The west wall near the mouth of the cove offers a colorful assortment of invertebrates at 30 to 60ft.

After fertilizing the eggs, male cabezon will guard a nest until the eggs hatch.

Anyone who's dived in Northern California for long will tell you that the diving in Carmel Bay is beautiful and exciting. Those who have been lucky enough to dive south of Point Lobos claim that the diving improves as you travel farther south along the Big Sur coast.

The Big Sur coast is characterized by sheer cliffs that drop vertically to the water. Beneath the water's surface, the bottom continues to plunge. Access to dive sites is the biggest challenge facing divers in this area. A few sandy beaches tucked away along the rugged coast offer shore access to some dive sites, but only for the very fit. Plus, the only way to reach these beaches by car is to follow the winding curves of Highway 1. In a practical sense, access is limited to boat dives, most of which are advanced dives on jagged pinnacles and rocky finger reefs. The closest harbor and boat launch facility of any size is in Monterey Bay to the north.

Sheer cliffs plunge below the water.

The excellent visibility is one big advantage this area has over Monterey Bay (and sometimes even Carmel Bay). Limited run-off results in exceptionally clear water by California standards. Visibility is rarely less than 40ft (12m) and sometimes exceeds 80ft (24m). This section of the coast, which has seen few divers over the years, also offers bigger fish and a greater abundance of fish, scallops and colorful invertebrates.

## Big Sur Coast Dive Sites

| | Good Snorkeling | Novice | Intermediate | Advanced |
|---|---|---|---|---|
| 23 Yankee Point | | | | ● |
| 24 Lobos Rock | | | ● | |
| 25 Soberanes Point | | | ● | |
| 26 Diablo Pinnacles | | | ● | |
| 27 Jade Cove | | ● | | ● |

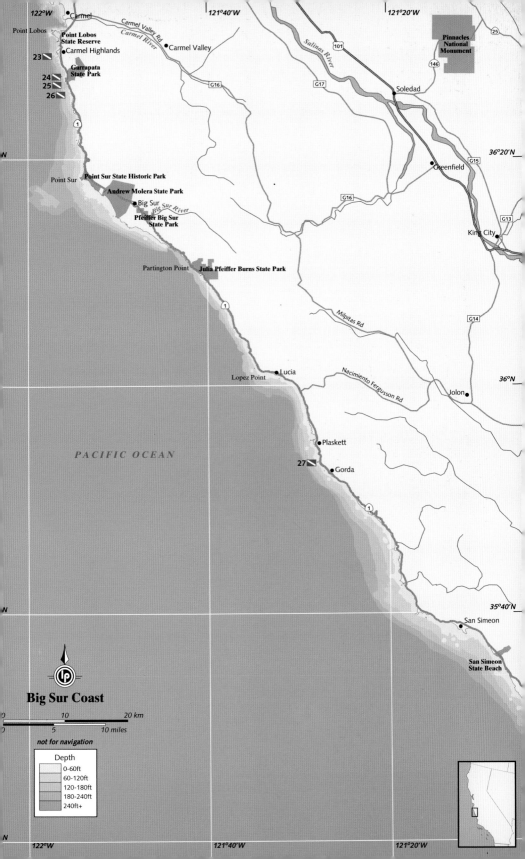

Big Sur Coast

0          10            20 km
0     5           10 miles

*not for navigation*

Depth
0-60ft
60-120ft
120-180ft
180-240ft
240ft+

## 23 Yankee Point

The California Department of Fish and Game has deemed Yankee Point the official dividing line between Northern and Southern California shores. The primary difference between the two regions relates to the taking of abalone—the law indicates that no tanks can be used north of Yankee Point, but tanks can be used to take abalone south of this point. However, due to declining abalone populations, there is currently a moratorium (for an indefinite time period) on the taking of *any* abalone south of San Francisco. If the moratorium is lifted, then the existing regulation regarding the use of tanks comes into effect.

Yankee Point can be accessed only by boat. One of the best areas to dive is a huge granite seamount that reaches up

**Location:** 2 miles (3.2km) south of Point Lobos

**Depth Range:** 50-100+ft (15-30+m)

**Access:** Boat

**Expertise Rating:** Advanced

to within 50ft of the surface about a half mile offshore. The top of the seamount resembles a plateau, with steep-walled canyons cut into its sides. The rocky surfaces are decorated with colorful invertebrates, including cobalt sponges, coralline algae, pink and orange strawberry anemones and a variety of tealia anemones. Large schools of blue rockfish can be found floating back and forth above the reef. You'll find myriad rockfish, such as the black-and-yellow rockfish, china rockfish, tree rockfish, blunt nosed sculpins, cabezon and lingcod, which hide among the cuts and crevices of the reef. This is one of the few areas outside of Southern California where chestnut cowries can be found. Many magnificent nudibranchs also populate this area.

On the inshore side of the plateau there is a relatively flat sandy bottom at 90 to 100ft. On the ocean side, vertical walls drop to ledges that terrace downward from 120ft into the depths. Divers should pay close attention to their time and depth. This area is exposed to northwest swells and can often become very rough. Offshore currents can also pose a hazard.

Lingcod hide in crevices at Yankee Point.

# 24  Lobos Rocks

Lobos Rocks is about 1,000 yards west of Moby Ling Cove, which is just north of Soberanes Point. Two pinnacles protrude 15 to 20ft above the surface, depending upon the tides. Some of the best diving is found on the inshore side of the inner pinnacle, where a sheer vertical wall drops to the flat, rocky seafloor at 90ft. You'll find white metridium anemones covering this wall from 50ft down.

A relatively shallow reef ridge extends south from the inner pinnacle. The top of the reef is at approximately 40ft. A thick kelp bed, composed mostly of giant kelp, rises from the top of the reef and a deep channel separates the reef from the shore. There is a distinct open area between the kelp beds that marks the channel. When it is calm, the visibility in this area can be exceptional, sometimes reaching 60 to 80ft.

The area between the pinnacles is seldom diveable because of the heavy surge.

**Location:** West of Moby Ling Cove

**Depth Range:** 25-90ft (7.6-27m)

**Access:** Boat

**Expertise Rating:** Intermediate

On rare days when the ocean is very flat, take the opportunity to explore this area. You'll find incredible carpets of unusually large pink, orange and lavender corynactis. A variety of large filter feeders, including acorn barnacles and colonial feather duster tube worms, live among the corynactis. There are also large tealia anemones and a scattering of pink and orange hydrocoral.

This area is exposed to prevailing northwest swells. Watch out for the extreme depths, hazardous heavy surge and strong offshore currents.

An acorn barnacle extends a feathery foot from its shell to filter plankton out of the water.

A diver makes a decompression stop beneath the kelp canopy.

## 25 Soberanes Point

Soberanes Point is approximately 4.8 miles south of Point Lobos on Highway 1. A grove of cypress trees on the east side of the road marks the parking areas (on both sides of the road). Two dirt paths lead to the beach access points. The path to the left goes to Soberanes Point and the path to the right leads to Moby Ling Cove. With scuba gear, the one-third mile trek is arduous at best. This area is difficult to enter and exit when the ocean is rough. Because it is such a long hike with tanks and weights, try this site only if you are in excellent physical condition and only on very calm days. Several commercial dive charters from Monterey Bay occasionally visit the kelp bed in this area, but only on extremely calm days.

The area between Soberanes Point and the offshore rocks has a mostly sandy bottom at 50 to 80ft, with many miniature pinnacles that rise 30 to 40ft off the bottom. Most rocky surfaces are entirely covered with algae and sponges,

**Location:** 4.8 miles (7.7km) south of Point Lobos

**Depth Range:** 25-80ft (7.6-24m)

**Access:** Shore or boat

**Expertise Rating:** Intermediate

and are littered with cowries, nudibranchs, anemones, crabs and barnacles. There is an abundance of fish, including lingcod, cabezon and black rockfish, and scallops and abalone can also be found.

**Moby Ling Cove** is just north of this area. Most of the cove is 30 to 50ft deep. On the north side of the cove there is a 40ft-wide underwater arch. Beyond the arch, the seafloor quickly slopes to a sandy bottom with rocky pinnacles. Yellow encrusting sponges, brightly colored corynactis, rose anemones and other invertebrates are abundant.

Moby Ling Cove, just north of Soberanes Point, is protected from the surf and surge.

Visibility often exceeds 75ft at Diablo Pinnacles.

## 26 Diablo Pinnacles

You'll find the two submerged seamounts of Diablo Pinnacles approximately 1 nautical mile due south of Soberanes Point and half a nautical mile offshore from the Granite Canyon Bridge. This is strictly a boat dive. In the spring and summer months the site is easily found by looking for a thick kelp bed.

The outside pinnacle comes to within 25ft of the surface and is relatively flat. The walls of the pinnacle drop to a 90ft rocky bottom on the inshore side and depths in excess of 100ft on the ocean

**Location:** 1 nautical mile south of Soberanes Point

**Depth Range:** 25-100+ft (7.6-30+m)

**Access:** Boat

**Expertise Rating:** Intermediate

side. The top of the pinnacle is cut with mini canyons, crevices and ledges full of hydrocorals and anemones. Marine life beneath the kelp canopy includes rockfish, crabs, cabezon, lingcod and an assortment of invertebrates. The visibility is often excellent because of the lack of runoff.

This area experiences frequent upwellings, which bring many deepwater animals—such as salps and jellyfish—to within diving depths. Divers should be wary of the usually strong currents.

## Salps

If a long, transparent creature floats by you along the California coast, you may be diving with a pelagic salp recently swept into diving depths by a cold upwelling. Salps are part of the subphylum Urochordata, which consists of chordate animals that do not have backbones. These animals, commonly called tunicates, can be solitary or colonial dwellers, and

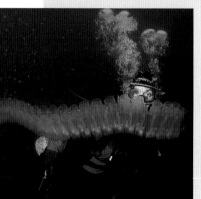

be either attached to the substrate or pelagic. Tunicates are among the most common marine invertebrates, but their many forms make them difficult to recognize. Many divers mistake stationary tunicates for sponges, and transparent pelagic tunicates for jellyfish.

Salps are solitary, pelagic tunicates that reproduce by budding. The parent salp divides asexually, forming a growth that becomes an individual bud. Each bud or link in the salp chain detaches and swims free when mature. Individual salps have elongated cylindrical bodies covered by a semi-transparent tunic. They pump water through their bodies to breathe, eat and move. They can't move very fast, but luckily they have few predators to swim away from.

## 27 Jade Cove

Jade Cove is actually two small coves found 8 miles south of Limekiln Campground, 10 miles south of Lucia and 65 miles south of Monterey. Jade Cove is marked by a sign on Highway 1, just south of Sand Dollar Beach and Plaskett Creek Campground. There is a fairly flat trail across the meadow to the top of a bluff overlooking the ocean. A steep switchback trail is the only access down to the northern cove. It is a difficult climb with tanks and weights. Wear sturdy shoes or booties with heavy soles, and a sure-footed mule or Sherpa might help.

The coves also can be accessed by inflatable. The nearest launching site

**Location:** 10 miles (16km) south of Lucia

**Depth Range:** 20-60ft (6.1-18m)

**Access:** Shore, or boat or inflatable

**Expertise Rating:** Advanced

is at Limekiln Campground. Watch out for big surf and surge when launching an inflatable from the beach. On the fairly long run from Limekiln to Jade Cove you often will see blue sharks basking at the surface.

Small pieces of jade often can be found on the gravel beach at Jade Cove.

Jade Cove's beach is wedged between massive rock formations and is composed of rocks and coarse gravel. This area is exposed to prevailing swells and can become quite rough. Only attempt this dive on calm days. Large veins of jade run into the sea from the two coves, and small jade stones can be found in the loose gravel underwater and in the exposed areas of the beach at low tide. Look for jade in the shallow water, but only on calm days, as the shallows are not diveable when it is rough. Storms often expose new pieces of jade.

Take a compass to navigate through the cove's thick kelp, which includes bull, featherboa, palm and giant kelps. The bottom has large boulders, rocks and gravel covered with red coralline algae. Divers will see lingcod, cabezon, painted greenlings, sculpins, nudibranchs, sponges and blue and black rockfish.

On the south side of the cove just 50 yards offshore is **Cave Rock**. There is a 30ft-long tunnel in 25ft of water at the base of this large wash rock. The tunnel runs through the rock, parallel to shore. A vein of polished jade is clearly visible on the inside rock face of the cave.

## Looking for Jade

Jade is the common term applied to two different minerals—nephrite and jadeite. Nephrite, popular in ancient China, is more difficult to fracture than jadeite, though it is not as hard and has a soapy appearance. Jadeite is more brilliant and usually has a higher value. Pure jade is white and, though green is most common, it can come in almost any color or even be nearly transparent or translucent. Nephrite is found in Jade Cove in various shades of green, and is very scratch resistant. Several types of rocks get tumbled in the surf of Jade Cove, making them smooth like jade. Because some of the jade is very dark, it is often hard to tell it from these other rocks without a scratch test.

### Regulations

A federal regulatory amendment permitting limited jade collecting went into effect in

1998. Jade can be taken from the area between southern Sand Dollar Beach south to Cape San Martin, from depths of up to 90ft (27m). Jade may not be collected above the mean high tide mark. Only loose jade pieces can be removed from the seabed. The only tools allowed are dive knives, abalone irons or pry bars no more than 36 inches (91cm) long. These tools can be used to maneuver or lift loose pieces or to scratch a rock to see if it is jade. The total combined capacity of jade collection bags can be no more than 200lbs (91kg), though the current limit appears to be 100lbs (46kg) per person. Any removal that would adversely affect the bottom habitat is not allowed.

Diver holds 10lb Jade Cove trophy.

Most of the dive sites along the Sonoma coast are between Fort Ross Reef Campground (11 miles or 18km north of Jenner) and Stewart's Point (about 28 miles or 45km north of Jenner). Free-diving is the most popular activity among sport divers in this region for two reasons. First, many divers are drawn to the Sonoma coast by the lure of abalone, which can only be taken without the use of tanks. Second, access to most of the good spots requires a long hike—reason enough for most divers to leave their heavy gear behind. There are, however, a few spots that are easily accessible to people with scuba gear, and to those who prefer to boat dive. Timber Cove, Stillwater Cove and Salt Point State Park's Gerstle Cove are all fairly well protected from northwest swells and have launching areas suitable for small inflatables. Timber Cove has a small dive store and is the best launching facility in the county.

The ocean temperatures are usually 48 to 52°F (9 to 11°C). Though the Sonoma coast is a bit colder than Monterey, most divers don't notice because they work a lot harder free-diving than they would scuba diving. Visibility is often limited to no more than a dirty 5 or 10ft (1.5 to 3m). When visibility drops even further, abalone diving is like diving by Braille. What most divers see is murky water, kelp, rocks and (sometimes) abalone. Few have time to even look at anything else while holding their breath. This is unfortunate, because colorful and fascinating creatures live on or near the bottom.

Gerstle Cove offers a protected gravel beach entry that is often used for classes.

## Sonoma Coast Dive Sites

| | Good Snorkeling | Novice | Intermediate | Advanced |
|---|---|---|---|---|
| **28 Pidotti Ranch** | ● | ● | | |
| **29 Fort Ross Reef Campground** | ● | | ● | |
| **30 Fort Ross State Historic Park** | ● | ● | | |
| **31 Cemetery Reef** | | | | ● |
| **32 Timber Cove** | ● | ● | | |
| **33 Stillwater Cove** | ● | ● | | |
| **34 Ocean Cove** | ● | | ● | |
| **35 Salt Point State Park** | ● | ● | | |

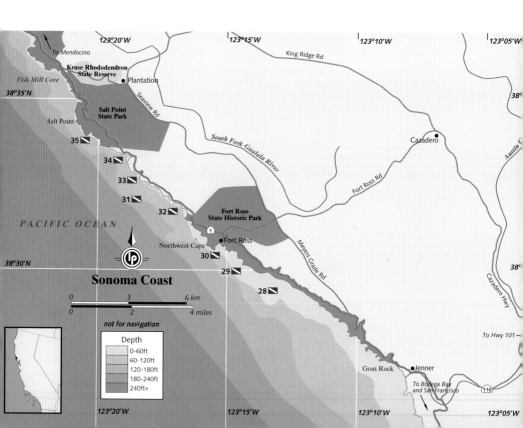

# The Elusive Red Abalone

The abalone is a large mollusk with a single bowl-shaped shell and a heavy, muscular foot that it uses to attach to the rocky substrate. Abalone feed on kelp, so if you find a thick, plush kelp bed, you can bet on finding one or more of these gastropods.

Nearly all of the abalone in northern California are red abalone (*Haliotis rufescens*). There are also a very few black abalone (*Haliotis cracherodii*, a candidate for the endangered species list) and pintos (*Holiotis kamtschatkana*, a hybrid). The delicate flavor of red abalone has made it one of the most highly prized—and highly priced—catches. Red abalone are still fairly abundant in shallow water along the coast from Jenner to Fort Bragg and beyond but (despite heavy regulation) commercial and sport collection have made finding legal-size abalone increasingly difficult.

## Abalone Diving Regulations

California law requires all game divers to have a fishing license, issued by the California Department of Fish and Game, and available through diving and sporting goods stores. As of 1998, you must add a sport abalone stamp to your fishing license in order to take abalone.

The abalone season extends from April 1 to June 30, and from August 1 to November 30. The law indicates that scuba cannot be used to take abalone north of Yankee Point (Monterey County), but can be used south of this point. However, there is a moratorium (for an indefinite time period) on the taking of *any* abalone south of San Francisco. If the moratorium is lifted, the existing regulation regarding the use of tanks comes into effect.

Divers are not allowed to remove a red abalone that's less than 7 inches (18cm) long, determined by measuring the maximum diameter of the shell. What's more, the maximum number of abalone that can be removed each day is four per person. Check with the Department of Fish and Game for any changes to the law.

## Abalone Diving Tips

Measure the abalone before removing it to ensure that it's large enough to take. Fish and Game regulations require that you measure abalone with an ab gauge or properly marked ab iron. (An abalone gauge is solely a measuring device. An ab iron is primarily used to remove abalone.) Another way to measure abs is to hold your gloved hand over the shell with your fingers and thumb spread. If you can't see the shell extending beyond the tips of both your thumb and little finger, it's probably too small. Remember, if you touch an abalone it will clamp down on the rocky bottom, making it very difficult to remove.

Once you find a legal-size abalone, slowly insert about 2 to 3 inches (5 to 8cm) of the ab iron between the rock and the mollusk's foot. Pull the handle up and away from the rock so that the end of the iron presses against the rock, and the middle of the iron pries the side of the shell away from the rock. Be careful not to cut the abalone in case you discover upon removing it that it's too small to keep. Though you may be well intentioned by returning an undersized ab to the bottom, a badly cut abalone can bleed to death. Also, be sure that it is returned with its foot down. Normally, an abalone can reattach itself to a rock after you pry it off, but it will be at the mercy of nearby predators if it settles on its back.

## 28 Pidotti Ranch

Pidotti Ranch is also known to many as "Red Barn," named after the barns (now painted white) just north of the parking area. This area is just south of Fort Ross Reef Campground.

**Location:** 10 miles (16km) north of Jenner

**Depth Range:** 10-15ft (3-4.6m)

**Access:** Shore

**Expertise Rating:** Novice

The hike to the beach is long. Two access trails—one to the north and the other to the south—lead across a meadow to the edge of the bluff and then down to the cove. The switchback trail at the north end provides the easiest access to the beach from the top of the bluff. There is also a steep trail or dirt path to the beach from the south part of the bluff.

Abalone cling to rocks.

The cove itself has a narrow rocky beach. This site is exposed to the open ocean and has very limited visibility. The water usually has a milky appearance because of runoff and sediment. Palm kelp covers the reef thickly throughout the cove. The bottom consists of medium to small rocks. The water remains shallow for quite a distance from the beach: It is barely deeper than 10ft for more than 50 yards offshore. Abalone are plentiful, although on the small side. It is still quite easy for free-divers to catch their limit of legal-size abalone, but you'll find larger ones elsewhere along the coast.

## 29 Fort Ross Reef Campground

Fort Ross Reef Campground (formerly Red Barn State Park) is rarely visited by scuba divers but is a popular site among free-divers. This state park facility is 11 miles north of Jenner on Highway 1. There is a $5 day-use fee and a $12 fee for overnight camping. Two access roads start at the main gate. One allows you to park on the bluffs that rise some 60ft above the main beach. The other, which cuts through a ravine, takes you to a parking area at the north end of the cove. Campsites are tucked away on either side

**Location:** 11 miles (18km) north of Jenner

**Depth Range:** 10-50ft (3-15m)

**Access:** Shore or dive board

**Expertise Rating:** Intermediate

of the ravine. Each campsite has a picnic table and a cleared area suitable for a tent. Near the kiosk at the gate and throughout the camping area you'll find portable toilets and faucets with fresh water.

The dive site is in the wide crescent-shaped cove whose shoreline is made up of small pebbles instead of sand. You can get there both from the parking area at the end of the ravine and from the bluffs. The ravine entry is less demanding in that you won't have to carry your gear up and down the cliffs. However, the bluffs are much closer to the best diving area, which is found off the south end of the beach.

The bottom is shallow near the beach—it's less than 15ft deep for as far as a quarter mile offshore. On the south end of the beach, past the pinnacles that rise above the surface, the bottom is at 10 to 20ft, though crevices in the bottom make some areas much deeper. Here you'll

find schools of blue and black rockfish, kelp greenlings, deepwater vermilion or red rockfish, lingcod, olive rockfish and surfperch. This area is somewhat protected from the vicious storms coming out of the northwest, though you will encounter moderate to heavy surf and surge. The runoff from the mouth of the Russian River frequently reduces visibility.

Rockfish are difficult to identify because of their various color phases. Their color patterns and shape also change as they age.

## 30  Fort Ross State Historic Park

Fort Ross State Historic Park is on Highway 1, a mile north of the entrance to Fort Ross Reef Campground, 12 miles north of Jenner. In the early 19th century, Russian fur trappers built a fort and trading settlement on this site. The fort has been completely restored and is now a major tourist attraction. For divers, Fort Ross Cove offers great diving conditions when rough water and northwest swells rule out other dive areas along the north coast. Unfortunately, the visibility is usually not as good as it is elsewhere on the coast.

Fort Ross is actually home to two coves. The sand beach of the **South Cove**

**Location:** 12 miles (19km) north of Jenner

**Depth Range:** 10-60ft (3-18m)

**Access:** Shore, boat or dive board

**Expertise Rating:** Novice

provides a means to launch dive boards, kayaks and even small inflatables with sand wheels. There is not much to see right off the beach, so you'll need to swim a ways to reach the rocks on the outer edges of this cove.

The **North Cove** offers the best diving. A dirt trail leads to the northern end of the north cove from the road behind Fort Ross. You can drive to the bottom of the hill behind the fort and dump your gear, then park in the upper parking lot.

There's a large wash rock in the middle of North Cove. Lying directly in line with the wash rock and the beach you'll find the wreck of the *Pomona*. The ship, a 225ft-long deluxe passenger freighter built in 1888, went down in 1907 while making the trek between San Francisco and Eureka. Its remains are strewn over a large area in 15 to 25ft of water. Divers occasionally find portholes, fittings, parts of the huge mast, winches, boilers and other pieces of the ship. The entire wreck is within the boundaries of the state park and is protected: Do not remove anything.

Beyond the wash rock the bottom drops quickly to 50ft. Sediment covers just about everything except for the white metridium anemones on the rocky reef. There are several types of low-lying kelp, as well as rocks, sand, crabs, snails, chitons and algae. The best abalone diving is around the northern point, which is often too rough to dive. Another good place for abalone is around a rock pile on the north side of the beach, where the water is only 10ft deep and is usually calm.

Free-diver inspects an abalone at the surface.

## 31  Cemetery Reef

Cemetery Reef is a mile-long ridge that runs parallel to shore just north of Timber Cove. The reef was named after the small cemetery that overlooks the ocean here. The best diving is around the L-shaped plateau, which lies about 400 yards offshore, midway between Timber Cove and Stillwater Cove. The top of the reef, in 20 to 30ft of water, is carpeted with a dense layer of algae and strands of bull kelp. Large abalone are abundant on

**Location:** North of Timber Cove

**Depth Range:** 30-70ft (9.1-21m)

**Access:** Boat

**Expertise Rating:** Advanced

the reeftop and are well within the range of most free-divers.

The nearly vertical sides of the reef drop to a jumble of massive boulders and rocks between 40 and 70ft. Brightly colored encrusting sponges, colonies of corynactis, large acorn barnacles and metridium anemones cover the walls, making a spectacular backdrop for photographing divers and fish. Expect to find large lingcod, cabezon and sea trout making their way through the maze of cracks and crevices formed by the boulders and rocks.

The visibility is often better here than in areas closer to the shore because of the strong currents. Be sure to check that your boat anchor is secure and leave plenty of slack in the line.

Colorful marine life adorns Cemetery Reef.

## 32 Timber Cove

Timber Cove is on Highway 1 about a mile north of Fort Ross State Historic Park and 13 miles north of Jenner. The main attraction is a large cove surrounded by high cliffs, which can be reached only by driving down a steep dirt road on private property. Timber Cove Boat Landing offers numerous amenities, including overnight camping, hot showers, washers and dryers, bait, tackle, a small dive store and a boat launch that can accommodate boats up to 18ft long. The owners charge a nominal fee to use the boat launch or for shore access. The boat launching facility provides access to many areas north of Timber Cove that can't be reached from shore.

The inside of the cove is generally protected from the prevailing ocean swells. The

**Location:** 13 miles (21km) north of Jenner

**Depth Range:** 10-40ft (3-12m)

**Access:** Shore, boat or dive board

**Expertise Rating:** Novice

A china rockfish stays close to the protection of a deep hole.

resulting onslaught of sport divers has depleted or driven away many of the fish and abalone that thrived here. Most of the year you can find abalone in the dense kelp beds north and south of the cove, which are also good spots for scuba diving and general sightseeing. It's tempting to swim all the way out around the north point of the cove to dive in the cluster of wash rocks, but this should be attempted only on exceptionally calm days.

Harbor seals frequently visit the main beach. You'll often see a young seal frolicking in the shallow waters, checking out the human activity on the beach, or waiting for handouts from divers who are cleaning fish. The seals that swim within the sheltered coves to the north of Timber Cove are a bit more aggressive. They've been known to steal fish off the stringers of spearfishing divers.

## 33 Stillwater Cove

Just 14 miles north of Jenner is Stillwater Cove, one of the Sonoma County Regional Parks. The campground, just south of the cove and off of Highway 1, functions on a first-come, first-served basis. The facilities include restrooms, showers, campsites and space for campers or trailers.

You can use the few 15-minute parking spaces just inside the park entrance for loading and unloading gear. Small inflatables can be launched across the sand and pebble beach, but since you can't park with trailered boats in the 15-minute spaces, you literally have to pull boats in by hand (i.e., on sand wheels

**Location:** 14 miles (23km) north of Jenner

**Depth Range:** 10-40ft (3-12m)

**Access:** Shore, dive board or inflatable

**Expertise Rating:** Novice

from the street entrance) if you want to launch here. Dive boards also are used to reach areas beyond swimming distance. You'll find a few more parking spaces along the road on the south side of the cove, and a steep switchback dirt path leading down to the beach below.

As you may have guessed from the name, this site is well protected from strong currents and wave action. In fact, Stillwater Cove is just about the only place where you can get into the water during high seas, a major reason why this cove is used for basic scuba instruction.

The middle of the cove is marked by fairly rugged and barren terrain, so freedivers will want to head north or south. For good scuba diving, head straight out from the beach until the bottom drops to

Giant green anemones withstand strong surf.

50ft. Visibility is not usually good in the areas closest to the beach, but the water becomes clearer about 75 to 100 yards from shore. In addition to low-lying kelp, a rocky bottom and algae, you will see green anemones, crabs, tealia anemones, cup corals, cabezon, kelp greenling, nudibranchs and sea stars.

## 34 Ocean Cove

Ocean Cove is a privately owned bluff and beach that has been developed extensively over the past few years. Facilities include campsites, toilets, showers and changing rooms, potable water and a gas station. Pay the $5 day-use and $12 camping fees at the Ocean Cove grocery store, across the road from the entrance gate. You can get airfills at the portable air station on weekends from April through November (Saturdays 10am to 5pm and Sundays 9am to 12pm). If you plan on diving this area during the winter, you can often arrange for airfills through the grocery store (☎ 707-847-3422). Ask for Captain Bob.

The entrance to Ocean Cove is at mile-marker SON 38.00, at a sharp curve along Highway 1. Once inside the main gate you'll see a fork in the road. The

**Location:** 15 miles (24km) north of Jenner

**Depth Range:** 10-50ft (3-15m)

**Access:** Shore, dive board or inflatable

**Expertise Rating:** Intermediate

road to the right leads to a bluff that overlooks the main beach. Here there is a parking lot, restrooms, a fish-cleaning station and a road that leads down to a rocky beach where divers can launch small inflatable boats and kayaks.

The left road goes to the cliffs at the south point of the cove. You can access some of the better dive sites via the steep

Divers launch inflatables from the rocky shore of Ocean Cove.

path covered with loose sand: It is not an easy task to haul your gear up and down the cliff, but well worth the effort.

The best diving begins at the large wash rock near the south point of the cove. The south wall at the point and the area just outside of the point are excellent spots to look for abalone. You can find "glory holes" (small pockets in the bottom filled with abalone) in less than 15ft of water. Some of the deep holes in this area drop below 50ft. The kelp bed around the southern point is dense most of the year and may pose a problem for free-divers, so be careful.

The center of the cove has several rocky pinnacles that rise almost to the surface. This area is rocky, with many cracks and crevices hiding good-sized abalone in depths of less than 20ft. On rough days, you can still usually dive this area.

Just outside the north point of the cove you'll find numerous and sizable fish, such as lingcod, black rockfish, cabezon and kelp greenlings on the reef. The north point is too far to swim from shore, so plan on getting there by boat or dive board. Because Ocean Cove is exposed to northwest swells, the water can become very rough.

## 35 | Salt Point State Park

You'll find Salt Point State Park off Highway 1 at mile-marker 40. There is a day-use fee of $5 to enter the park. The facilities include restrooms (at both Gerstle and South Gerstle Coves), outdoor showers, changing rooms and a fish-cleaning station. The three campgrounds offer many campsites, and require reservations from April through October.

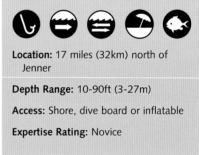

**Location:** 17 miles (32km) north of Jenner

**Depth Range:** 10-90ft (3-27m)

**Access:** Shore, dive board or inflatable

**Expertise Rating:** Novice

Upwellings often bring jellyfish to the surface.

Gerstle Cove and South Gerstle Cove are the most popular dive sites at Salt Point.

**Gerstle Cove**, a designated reserve, is the main dive site in the park. A paved road leads down to the Gerstle Cove beach, where divers can launch small boats or dive boards. This is also a good entry point for swimming out with surf mats, tubes or floats. The surf is typically light to moderate, and you'll find calm to moderate surge except when there are monster swells.

The depth inside the cove ranges from 10 to 40ft. The bottom is rock strewn with boulders of various sizes on sloping sand. At the mouth of the cove the water is about 50ft deep, then drops off steeply to 80ft or more. Large numbers of nudibranchs, chitons, strawberry anemones and a variety of sea stars and other creatures make the cove a great place for macrophotography. Though no fish or abalone can be taken from within the cove, the extensive kelp beds outside the cove are good spots for abalone hunting, spearfishing and sightseeing.

Water conditions at **South Gerstle Cove** are usually rougher than in the reserve, but access is still fairly easy except on days when the ocean is particularly rough. Several trails lead from the dirt access road down to rocky shore entries. In the center of the cove the trail access is easiest, but it is a longer swim to the good abalone areas, found at the mouth of the cove and to the right, outside the north edge of South Gerstle Cove at 15 to 30ft deep. This is almost solely an abalone diving area with little else to see except kelp and rocks.

Two other coves have been added to Salt Point State Park: **Stump Beach** and **Fisk Mill Cove**. Both areas are exposed to the elements, with dangerous surf and limited visibility. On calm days the diving, especially for abalone, can be quite good along the northern points of these coves.

Hermissenda nudibranchs are abundant.

## The Farallon Islands

The Farallon Islands are 27 miles (43km) off the coast west of San Francisco, in the Gulf of the Farallones National Marine Sanctuary. The water surrounding these small islands contains a vibrant and healthy marine environment teeming with fish, invertebrates, whales, sea birds, dolphins, sea lions and seals. From time to time divers are drawn to this area to explore and photograph this incredibly rich ecosystem.

Divers are not the only ones that find the marine life appealing. Great white sharks are attracted to the vicinity by the seals and sea lions, making this one of just three areas worldwide known to have a resident population of this infamous predator.

Great white sharks are known to be territorial, and watersports enthusiasts should be aware of possible dangers. On more than one occasion divers, surfers and others in the water have been attacked. For this reason, the area bordered by Point Reyes to the north, Half Moon Bay to the south and the Farallon Islands to the west has become known as the "Red Triangle."

KEN HOWARD

The Mendocino coast is north of the Sonoma coast. From Navarro River Beach north on Highway 1, the two-lane road winds along the scenic coastline, offering spectacular views of sea, surf, sheltered coves and rocky promontories. Although the Mendocino coast is not densely populated, it still attracts many divers, especially during abalone season (from April 1 through November 30, excluding July). Most of the accessible and interesting dive sites are along the northern half of the Mendocino coast, from Point Arena to Fort Bragg. You can launch boats from a ramp at Albion Flats and from Point Arena (with a hoist). There is also a private and a public launch ramp at Noyo Harbor at the south end of Fort Bragg.

Many of the spectacular underwater pinnacles along the Mendocino coast rival even the best diving that Carmel Bay offers. A variety of invertebrates add color and interest to the rocky outcrops. Walls of metridium anemones thrive on the offshore reefs. China rockfish and vermilion rockfish, which are rare in other areas, are commonplace. Water temperatures are typically 49 to 54°F (9 to 12°C), but can get as cold as 46°F (8°C).

| Mendocino Coast Dive Sites | Good Snorkeling | Novice | Intermediate | Advanced |
|---|:---:|:---:|:---:|:---:|
| 36 Anchor Bay | ● | | ● | |
| 37 Arena Rock | | | | ● |
| 38 Nowhere Reef | | | | ● |
| 39 Navarro River Beach | ● | | ● | |
| 40 Bull Rock | | | | ● |
| 41 Albion River Flats | ● | | ● | |
| 42 Colby Reef | | | | ● |
| 43 Van Damme State Park | ● | ● | | |
| 44 Blow Hole | ● | ● | | |
| 45 Jack Peters Gulch | ● | ● | | |
| 46 Russian Gulch State Park | ● | ● | | |

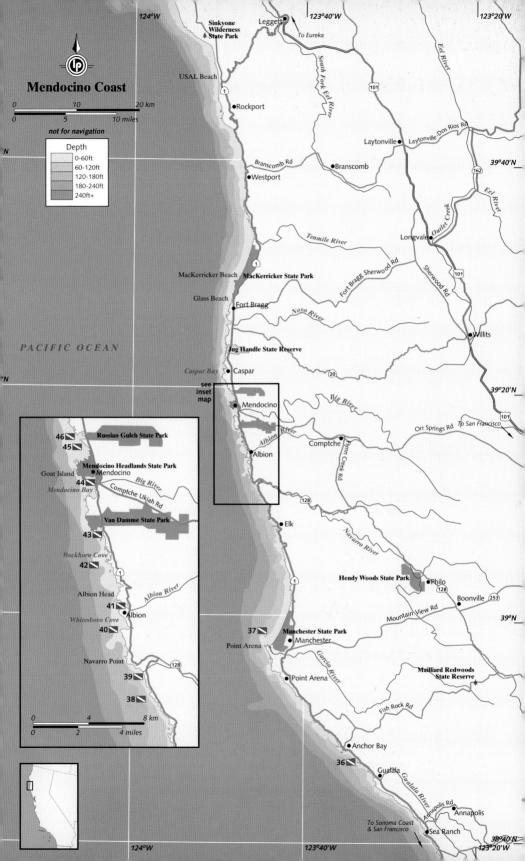

## 36 Anchor Bay

Anchor Bay is a privately owned campground and a beach access point at Fish Rock Beach. Facilities include campsites (most with electricity and water), restrooms and showers. With a grocery store, laundromat and restaurants nearby, Anchor Bay is ideal for family camping. The campground charges a nominal day-use fee.

**Location:** 1 mile (1.6km) north of Gualala

**Depth Range:** 10-60ft (3-18m)

**Access:** Shore, boat, dive board or inflatable

**Expertise Rating:** Intermediate

The best diving is at the north end of the ¾-mile-long beach. Whenever the surf is moderate to rough within the cove, so is the surge. During the summer and fall months, you can launch a small- to medium-sized inflatable across the sand

Rockfish find shelter in Anchor Bay's crevices.

at the north end of the cove. From there, a channel between the north wall of the cove and several wash rocks leads to an area called **Fish Rock**, just outside the point. Dive boards can also be used to reach Fish Rock, but it is too far to swim.

Beyond Fish Rock, the bottom drops steeply to a plateau in about 40ft of water, then drops off into progressively deeper water across a series of cuts that run roughly north to south. You can find schools of blue and black rockfish here, along with cabezon and lingcod. The bottom hosts platoons of sea stars, box crabs, nudibranchs and, in 60ft of water, white metridium anemones.

## 37 Arena Rock

Arena Rock, without question, is one of the premiere dive destinations on the north coast. This spectacular dive site is at the north end of Point Arena Cove, approximately 1½ miles north of the Point Arena Lighthouse and 15.4 nautical miles south of Albion Cove. You can access this site by launching a boat using the hoist at Point Arena Cove Pier, or by boat from Albion Flats. You also can launch inflatables at the small boat ramp to the left of the pier at Point Arena Cove.

**Location:** Approximately 1½ miles (2.4km) offshore from Point Arena

**Depth Range:** 22-100+ft (6.7-30+m)

**Access:** Boat or inflatable

**Expertise Rating:** Advanced

To get there from Highway 1, turn west on Port Road south of mile-marker 15.24

and follow the road to the pier. The facilities at the pier include restrooms and pay showers.

This site can be dived only on rare days when the ocean is extremely calm. Currents can be unpredictable and often turn into raging torrents. The north end of the cove offers some protection from the surf and surge, and can be a nice dive on relatively calm days. This area is full of shallow canyons running north to south where you are likely to find lingcod, rockfish and abalone.

About a mile offshore, a single pinnacle rises from the seafloor to within 22ft of the surface. Palm kelp and scattered strands of bull kelp cling to the top of the seamount and to some of the ledges down to about 45ft. Start your dive on the east side of this pinnacle and descend around the edge of the wall to the southeast corner. The south and southeast walls are pockmarked from 50ft to 120ft with undercuts, ledges, caves and tunnels big enough for divers to swim through.

Clouds of schooling fish and juvenile rockfish float around the rocky surfaces.

You'll see splashes of color everywhere. Metridiums, orange and pink strawberry anemones, encrusting sponges, large acorn barnacles and nudibranchs cover the walls and interior surfaces. There are pockets in the reef full of 7- to 8-inch rock scallops. Lingcod, vermilion rockfish and china rockfish inhabit every hole in the reef. Divers frequently will encounter 6- to 7-foot wolf eels curled up on the deep ledges. Jellyfish and salps often can be found in large numbers flowing over the top of the reef.

Large rock scallops are plentiful at Arena Rock.

## 38 Nowhere Reef

Nowhere Reef is an underwater pinnacle 1 nautical mile south of Navarro River Beach and one-half nautical mile west of Saddle Point. Appropriately named, this dive "in the middle of nowhere" is one of the most interesting sites in Northern California. This is normally a boat dive, but experienced divers may be able to reach it by dive board or kayak from Navarro River Beach. It is diveable only on calm days and often experiences heavy currents.

The top of the reef comes to within 18ft of the surface. Two deep, parallel

**Location:** 1 nautical mile due south of Navarro River Beach

**Depth Range:** 18-100+ft (5.5-30+m)

**Access:** Boat, dive board, kayak or inflatable

**Expertise Rating:** Advanced

cuts cross the top of this seamount north to south, forming three miniature pinnacles with sheer vertical walls. The bottoms of the cuts are between 75 and 80ft deep. The reeftop on the western-most pinnacle is only 20 to 25ft deep and is covered with a thick forest of bull kelp. Begin and end the dive in this area. The tops of the other two pinnacles are in 50 to 60ft of water.

Metridium anemones and orange corynactis cover the interior walls of these narrow canyons. At the bottom of the first cut (between the west and middle pinnacles), there is a swim-through adjacent to the eastern wall. The southern side of the pinnacle terraces to depths well below 100ft. Divers will find schools of blue rockfish, china rockfish, vermilion rockfish and lingcod. Nudibranchs, including large yellow and white dorids, are quite plentiful.

This nudibranch's colorful cerata contain stinging cells.

## 39 Navarro River Beach

Navarro River Beach is at the junction of Highway 1 and Highway 128, at the mouth of the Navarro River. Camping is allowed near the beach on the south side of the river mouth. There is a gravel parking area next to the ten camping sites, and the only facilities are pit toilets. Unfortunately there is no running water. To get to the camping area, turn

**Location:** 4 miles (6.4km) south of Albion River Flats

**Depth Range:** 5-35ft (1.5-11m)

**Access:** Shore, boat or dive board

**Expertise Rating:** Intermediate

west at the south end of the Navarro River Bridge.

The beach affords an excellent place to launch a kayak or small inflatable with sand wheels. The surf is generally moderate, and the area should not be dived when it gets rough. A number of small coves to the north across the river mouth are good for exploring, abalone diving and hunting, and the river is great for kayaking.

Navarro River Beach is primarily visited by free-divers. Straight out from the

Watch out for urchins at Navarro River Beach.

center of the beach is a wide, shallow shelf that extends from shore to an offshore reef. In the shallow water up to 75 yards from shore, the ocean water mixes with fresh water from the Navarro River, causing extremely poor visibility. Outside of this area, visibility improves. A series of rock piles in 10 to 20ft of water is home to a host of abalone.

Toward the north side of the beach is another reef where large 9-inch abalone are common. Outside this north break-

er, the walls of isolated pinnacles drop vertically from the surface to about 20ft. Finger canyons extend toward the open ocean and drop down to 35ft. The north wall, above the mouth of the river, is another prime abalone spot, as well as a home to rock scallops and large urchins. Large schools of blue and black rockfish are common outside the wash rocks on the north side of the beach, near the rock below the surface called "Navarro Arch."

## 40  Bull Rock

Whitesboro Cove, a large cove south of Albion and adjacent to the Salmon Creek Bridge, has a fairly shallow rocky bottom and is covered with a thick kelp bed throughout most of the year. Offshore from Whitesboro Cove is Bull Rock, a massive underwater pinnacle just half a nautical mile west of the Salmon Creek Bridge. This area is accessible by boat only. As is the case with most outer pinnacles, Bull Rock is diveable only on those days when the ocean is calm. Moderate to heavy currents are common at this site.

Bull Rock's pinnacle comes to within 18ft of the surface and drops to 135ft on the outside. This seamount is actually split into two mini pinnacles, with a saddle in the middle that drops to 104ft. Lingcod often litter the bottom of this saddle and abalone are plentiful. Billowy white metridium

**Location:** ½ nautical mile south of the buoy outside Albion Cove

**Depth Range:** 18-100+ft (5.5-30+m)

**Access:** Boat

**Expertise Rating:** Advanced

Metridium anemones cover much of the reef at Bull Rock and other offshore pinnacles.

anemones cover the interior walls of the pinnacle. Beneath stands of bull kelp and the smaller palm kelp, the rocky walls are also covered with corynactis, tealia anemones, brightly colored encrusting sponge and coralline algae. As you go deeper, you will find more large, white metridium anemones and rock scallops. The underwater terrain offers narrow canyons, steep walls and a myriad of cracks and crevices hiding lingcod, greenlings and cabezon. Several varieties of dorid nudibranchs can be found on this reef.

## 41  Albion River Flats

Albion Cove is at the mouth of the Albion River, at mile-marker 43.93 on Highway 1, approximately 4 miles south of the town of Mendocino. Albion River Flat is a large, private campground adjacent to the mouth of the Albion River. The campsites are on a flat grassy area, just east of the Albion River Bridge. The facilities include ample parking, pay showers, a fish-cleaning area and a small grocery store/café. The other Albion River campground, Schooner's Landing, is a mile farther upriver. To reach either campground, turn east at the north end of the bridge and take the road down to the camps. For a nominal day-use fee, the owners will allow you to launch

**Location:** 4 miles (6.4km) south of Mendocino

**Depth Range:** 10-60ft (3-18m)

**Access:** Shore, dive board, kayak or inflatable

**Expertise Rating:** Intermediate

kayaks and boats even if you don't have a campsite. A dive store at Schooner's Landing offers 1- and 2-tank dive charters and airfills. For information contact Dive Crazy Adventures.

Realistically, you need a boat or kayak to dive at Albion. At the north end of the cove there is an island that breaks up incoming swells from the northwest, keeping that end of the cove fairly calm. You'll find massive granite reefs with tunnels, narrow canyons and vertical walls adorned with colorful invertebrates. Beyond the cove's protective north point the water is often too rough to dive.

Inflatables are easy to launch from the beach at Albion Cove.

You can swim out from the beach under the Albion River Bridge and find abalone along the north shore of Albion Cove. Just outside of the bridge in the center of the boat channel is a group of rock piles in 20 to 30ft. The piles have an abundance of abalone but boat traffic can make the area dangerous for divers. The center of the cove has a sand bottom and slopes gradually toward deeper water.

On the south side of the cove at 30 to 60ft, scuba divers will find large boulders, cracks and crevices that attract numerous blue and black rockfish and cabezon. Several large anchors in the area are a testament to the many ships that have been wrecked along this shore.

## 42 Colby Reef

There are two pinnacles in this area. The southern pinnacle is named Colby Reef (though it is referred to as True Colby) and the northern pinnacle is aptly named Colby North. **True Colby** is 1 mile west of Stillwell Point and 2 miles south of Van Damme State Park. The top of the reef is a wide, flat plateau covered with bull kelp and palm kelp. The top sits at 30 to 40ft and causes the surface of the ocean to break on rough days.

The east side of the reef slopes gradually to 85ft. The north and west sides of the reef have vertical walls that plummet to 135ft. Fluffy white metridiums adorn the north wall. On the northwest wall, a tunnel penetrates the pinnacle from a cut at 95ft that opens into a large cavern within the pinnacle. There is a larger entrance to the same cavern on the east wall. The pinnacle is configured so that the tunnel is not very long, but it does penetrate from one side to the other. It is unlikely you would become disoriented inside because the cavern is not large. Divers will find schools of blue rockfish, black rockfish and assorted red rockfish and sea trout. Numerous horizontal cracks in the walls afford protection to large lingcod. Divers also will find rock scallops nestled among colorful tealia anemones.

**Location:** 5 miles (8km) south of Mendocino

**Depth Range:** 35-100+ft (11-30m)

**Access:** Boat

**Expertise Rating:** Advanced

Diver explores Colby Reef's interior.

The other pinnacle half a mile north sometimes offers a slightly calmer dive. The top of **Colby North** is at 35ft and has sheer drop-offs on the north and west sides. Currents are usually strong in this area and the reef is diveable only on those days when the sea is calm. Although there is less color on either of the Colby pinnacles than at some of the sites to the south, the visibility is usually very good.

## 43  Van Damme State Park

The town of Little River is home to Van Damme State Park, just 4 miles north of Albion and 3 miles south of Mendocino at mile-marker 48.03. Van Damme offers the most-protected diving access point along the Mendocino coast. It's well equipped, too, with facilities that include campsites, restrooms, running water and showers. The large fern-filled canyon found conveniently near the campground is a nice place for a leisurely walk when dive conditions aren't good, or you can hike along the Little River to the pygmy forest.

Van Damme's beach and cove are across Highway 1 from the park entrance.

**Location:** 3 miles (4.8km) south of Mendocino

**Depth Range:** 5-50ft (1.5-15m)

**Access:** Shore, boat or dive board

**Expertise Rating:** Novice

Boulders scattered in the shallow water directly in front of the beach are home to an impressive variety of marine life, including some abalone. On the south side of the cove are two large, rocky islands called **Top Hat** and **Key Hole**. The

Van Damme is the most-protected beach entry on the north coast.

drop-offs on the outside of these islands and the rocky fingers on the north side of the cove provide good diving on days when the surf isn't too heavy.

The boat channel at the north end of the large cove is about 40 to 50ft deep with a sandy bottom. On the channel's sloping walls and among the wash rocks toward the middle of the cove, divers can easily find their limit of 8- to 8½- inch abalone in depths between 15 and 30ft. These areas can be reached by swimming out from the beach, but it is a long kick out and back.

If you have a small boat, dive board or kayak, you may want to explore the numerous coves to the south. They are well protected from weather and offer caves and tunnels. The water is generally clear in these coves.

## 44  Blow Hole

Blow Hole ranks as one of California's top macrophotography sites. You'll find it at Portuguese Beach in Mendocino Bay, on the south side of the Mendocino Headlands. Turn west onto Main Street from Highway 1 and keep going until the road takes a forced right turn onto Heeser Street. There is usually ample parking along the side of the road. Walk through the gate on the left and follow the dirt path to the bluff overlooking the beach. A stairway fashioned from railway ties affords a relatively easy path to the beach. However, the 75 steps can be difficult in full gear, including tanks and weights. Because the dive is shallow, you can use a 50- or 63-cubic-foot tank, which is lighter and easier to carry and still will provide plenty of air.

On the right (west) side of the flat sandy beach there is a large, half-submerged tunnel that goes all the way through the bluff. The blow-hole, a large natural hole in the ceiling, allows lots of light to penetrate into the center of the tunnel. The water level is 10 to 20ft depending on the tides. It is a good idea to stay away from the ocean side of the tunnel on rough days because of the

**Location:** Main St. and Heeser St., Mendocino

**Depth Range:** 10-30ft (3-9.1m)

**Access:** Shore, boat or dive board

**Expertise Rating:** Novice

wave action and heavy surge, but the interior is almost always protected.

The mouth of the tunnel is only a few feet deep and is usually clogged with bull

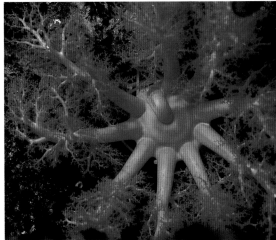

Sea cucumbers eat by licking their fingers.

kelp and featherboa kelp. Divers will find literally hundreds of nudibranchs on the floor and walls of the tunnel. Up to 30

Beautiful white-lined nudibranchs captivate photographers at the Blow Hole.

varieties can be seen on a single dive, including rare rose-colored white-lined nudibranchs, thick-horned aeolid nudibranchs and large orange-tipped nudibranchs. Other macro subjects include unusual bright-red sea cucumbers, many varieties of anemones, decorator crabs and sailfin sculpins.

In the center of the tunnel, under the blowhole itself, you'll see piles of old gears and other pieces of the pulleys and hoists once used to transport people and cargo from ships anchored offshore.

The middle of the cove is 20 to 30ft deep. Here you will likely see kelp (palm, featherboa and brown kelp), abalone, sea stars and anemones. This site is very protected and is frequently used for classes. The most serious hazards are the possibility of being tangled in the thick kelp or caught in the surge, dangers that careful divers can easily avoid.

## 45　Jack Peters Gulch

Jack Peters Gulch is a lesser-known dive site that is a great scuba dive, as well as a good free-dive. The site is 1 mile north of Mendocino (just north of the Mendocino Headlands). From Highway 1, turn west onto Road 500D (just north of Lansing Street). Take this road to the end, make a U-turn and park on the right. There is room for only three or four cars along the shoulder of the road, 0.8 miles after the turnoff. This site has no facilities, so bring your own water and whatever else you might need.

A dirt path leads toward the cliff overlooking the ocean. Where the pathway forks, stay to the right. The path will take

**Location:** 1 mile (1.6km) north of Mendocino

**Depth Range:** 10-40ft (3-12m)

**Access:** Shore

**Expertise Rating:** Novice

you to the water after only a short hike. There is a flat rocky area to the left of the small cove. Be careful walking over these extremely slippery rocks and climbing down to the water. Before starting your dive, look for the partially submerged cave on the far side of the cove. It is a good place to end a dive on a calm day.

Enter the water from the flat table rock and swim across the cove to the left of the cave. Begin your dive by turning toward the open ocean and descending on the other side of the cove's mouth. A myriad of channels wind their way through 30 to 50ft depths. When you leave the cove, follow the wall for about 30 yards. You should come across a long narrow tunnel that is almost enclosed. The bottom is at 40ft and the walls slant inward to a narrow opening at the top. Huge acorn barnacles adorn the walls of the tunnel. Throughout Jack Peters Gulch, pockets of abalone, large sunflower stars and a variety of colorful invertebrates cover the channel walls.

Save some air for the end of the dive. Return to the cove and take a peek into the cave opening seen from the surface. This is actually a huge tunnel that opens out into the back side of Russian Gulch. The bottom is only 20ft deep. The numerous side tunnels are well lit. Do this part of the dive only if it is extremely calm and you have plenty of air. If you take a close look at the rock surfaces, you will discover many large nudibranchs and a variety of sculpins and blennies hiding in cracks and crevices.

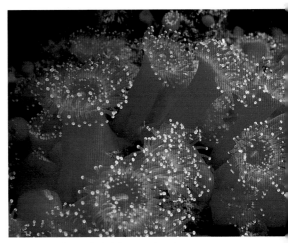

Lush carpets of strawberry anemones cover the caves and tunnels at Jack Peters Gulch.

Sculpins use camouflage to help them blend in with the surroundings.

## 46 Russian Gulch State Park

A clearly marked exit off Highway 1 points to Russian Gulch State Park, just north of the town of Mendocino and 10 miles south of Fort Bragg. The park offers camp sites, restrooms, hot showers and some of the most spectacular scenery on the north coast.

**Location:** Just north of Mendocino

**Depth Range:** 10-40ft (3-12m)

**Access:** Shore, boat or dive board

**Expertise Rating:** Novice

The park has a very protected beach entry and convenient parking. Small boats can be launched from the sandy beach into the main cove. Most divers enter the water in the main cove and dive just offshore or in the adjoining coves to the north and south. There is only a slight to moderate surge inside the cove, but it can be heavy outside.

A rocky entry is also available at the north point for more experienced divers. Novice and intermediate divers should stay away from this point, which is generally plagued with heavy swells and surge.

When the ocean is rough, the north point isn't diveable at all.

A group of small wash rocks lies on the south side of the main cove. You can almost always free-dive or scuba dive here, even when the sea is rough. This spot is also good for photography, as nudibranchs, sponges, anemones, abalone and rock scallops fill the rocky crevices. Legal (7-inch-long) abalone are quite plentiful here, though very few abalone are any bigger than that.

Russian Gulch State Park offers beautiful scenery typical of the Mendocino County.

# Northern Mendocino Free-Diving Sites

Many free-diving sites in northern Mendocino County are popular with visitors and locals alike. Some of these lesser-known sites are hard to get to, but often yield trophy abalone and other treasures.

**The Pipeline** is just one of many sites along the coast of the Mendocino headlands. To reach this area, turn west off Highway 1 onto Lansing Street and then right onto Hesser Street. You will pass another site (to your right) aptly named **The Bathrooms**. Stay on the road as it turns to the left, following the bluff. A dirt driveway leads to a parking lot overlooking the ocean and a path leads to the water's edge. This is a very good shore dive, with relatively easy (though rocky) access on calm days. The bottom drops to a series of channels between 10 and 40ft. The arches and caves are well appointed with colorful invertebrates and plenty of abalone.

"Abs" are abundant in Mendocino.

**Caspar Bay** has both beach and rock entries. The exit from Highway 1 to Caspar is clearly marked. Turn west onto Point Cabrillo Drive from Highway 1 at mile-marker 54.6. The free, public beach is at the bottom of the road. There are excellent beach dives and plenty of abalone in the cove to either side of the main beach. Facilities include campsites, a grocery store, hot showers and a laundromat. The Caspar Headlands State Reserve, a 5-acre area among private residences on the rocky south side of Caspar Bay, is a convenient non-beach entry for abalone diving. It is accessible from Headlands Drive, off of South Caspar Drive.

**Jug Handle State Reserve** is midway between Fort Bragg and Mendocino. Turn west off of Highway 1 at mile-marker 56. The facilities include pit toilets, fresh water, picnic tables and ample parking. Two separate beaches offer easy access for free-diving. There is reasonable diving for abalone along the north shore of the cove and near the wash rocks off the southern beach.

**Glass Beach** is an unusual site found near Fort Bragg. Turn west onto Elm Street. Park at the end of the road and hike a quarter-mile to the beach. This was the site of an old glass foundry, and was also the city dump until the 1960s. The beach here consists largely of colored bits of glass rather than sand. In the water, divers will find an assortment of rusted metal, including old engines and appliances, in addition to an abundance of red abalone.

**MacKerricker Beach State Park** is north of Fort Bragg on Highway 1. Turn west at mile-marker 64.90, drive through the campground and follow the road to the parking lot at the beach. The facilities include campsites, restrooms, showers and picnic tables. The north side of the beach is good for spearfishing. Because this is a popular area that sees large numbers of divers, the abalone are small except in depths below 25ft.

**USAL Beach** is a popular dive with locals, known as a great spot for 10 and 11 inch abs. Depths are variable, but you can find good shallow areas near shore and around the wash rocks. The area is difficult to get to and is for experienced divers only. Take a sharp turn west off Highway 1 at mile-marker 90.88 and go approximately 6 miles along the dirt and gravel road. There is a beach and primitive campground with pit toilets. You must bring your own food, water and supplies. It is suitable for shore diving, but a kayak allows you to cover more area. Kayaks can be launched from the beach.

# Marine Life

The nutrient-laden waters off the Central and Northern California coast offer divers one of the richest assemblages of marine life in the world. There are several thousand species of invertebrates alone. The diversity and color of the plants and animals found in this area is unmatched anywhere in the world.

This chapter provides images of some of the more common and interesting marine animals that California divers frequently encounter. Few of these animals pose any threat to divers. However, a short list of potentially hazardous marine life is included at the end of the chapter.

Common names are used freely but are notoriously inaccurate and inconsistent. The two-part scientific name, usually shown in italics, is more precise. It consists of a genus name followed by a species name. A genus is a group of closely related species that share common features. A species is a recognizable group within a genus whose members are capable of interbreeding. Where the species or genus is unknown, the naming reverts to the next known level: family (F), order (O), class (C) or phylum (Ph).

## Common Vertebrates

bat ray
*Myliobatis californica*

blackeye goby
*Coryphopterus nicholsii*

black-and-yellow rockfish
*Sebastes chrysomelas*

black rockfish
*Sebastes melanops*

blue rockfish
*Sebastes mystinus*

China rockfish
*Sebastes nebulosus*

gopher rockfish
*Sebastes carnatus*

tree rockfish (juvenile)
*Sebastes serriceps*

lingcod
*Ophiodon elongatus*

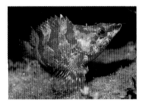

painted greenling
*Oxylebius pictus*

California scorpionfish (common
sculpin) *Scorpaena guttata*

coralline sculpin
*Artedius corallinus*

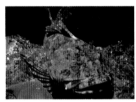

cabezon
*Scorpaenichthys marmoratus*

California halibut
*Paralichthys californicus*

wolf eel
*Anarrhichthys ocellatus*

California sea lion
*Zalophus californianus*

harbor seal
*Phoca vitulina*

sea otter
*Enhydra lutris*

## Common Invertebrates

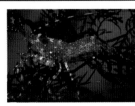

purple-ringed top shell
*Calliostoma annulatum*

sunflower star
*Pycnopodia helianthoides*

coonstripe shrimp
*Pandalus danae*

hermit crab
*Paguristes* sp.

purple jellyfish
*Pelagia panopyra*

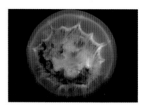

common (moon) jellyfish
*Aurelia aurita*

featherduster worm
*Eudistylia polymorpha*

white-plumed anemone
*Metridium senile*

tube anemone
*Pachycerianthus fimbriatus*

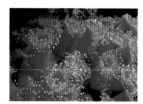

strawberry anemone
*Corynactis californica*

rose anemone
*Tealia piscivora*

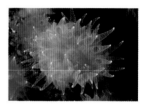

orange cup coral
*Balanophyllia elegans*

California sea hare
*Aplysia californica*

orange-tipped nudibranch
*Triopha catalinae*

sea lemon
*Anisodoris nobilis*

rainbow nudibranch
*Dendronotus irus*

white-lined nudibranch
*Dirona albolineata*

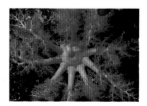

orange sea cucumber
*Cucumaria miniata*

Marine animals almost never attack divers, but many have defensive and offensive weaponry that can be triggered if they feel threatened or annoyed. The ability to recognize hazardous creatures is a valuable asset in avoiding accident and injury. The following are some of the potentially hazardous creatures most commonly found in Monterey Bay, Central and Northern California.

## Sea Urchins

Sea urchins tend to live in shallow areas near shore. They vary in coloration and size, with spines ranging from short and blunt to long and needle-sharp. The most common urchins in this region are the giant red sea urchin and the purple sea urchin. The spines are the urchin's most dangerous weapon, easily able to penetrate neoprene wetsuits, booties and gloves. Treat minor punctures by extracting the spines and immersing the wound in nonscalding hot water. More serious injuries require medical attention.

## Jellyfish

Jellyfish sting by releasing the stinging cells contained in their trailing tentacles. Because divers in Central and Northern California are covered head to toe (except for small areas around the mask), jellyfish stings in the water are unusual. The danger

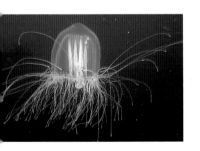

surfaces after divers touch the jellyfish with their gloves, transferring nematocysts from the tentacles that later come in contact with bare skin. Stings are often irritating and not painful, but should be treated immediately with a decontaminant such as vinegar, rubbing alcohol, baking soda, papain or dilute household ammonia. Beware that some people may have a stronger reaction than others, in which case you should prepare to resuscitate and seek medical aid.

## Scorpionfish

Scorpionfish are well-camouflaged creatures that have poisonous spines along their dorsal fins. They are often difficult to spot since they typically rest quietly on the bottom, looking more like rocks than fish. Although all rockfish are members of the family Scorpanidae (the scorpionfish), only the California scorpionfish or common sculpin (*Scorpaena guttata*) is capable of inflicting serious wounds. However, the spines of all rockfish can inflict painful punctures. Practice good buoyancy control and watch where you put your hands. To treat a puncture, wash the wound and immerse in nonscalding hot water for 30 to 90 minutes. Administer pain medications if necessary.

## Electric Rays

Electric rays can be found hovering over sand patches or partially buried in the sand. They have a rounded flat body that is blue-gray on top with a light underbelly. Unique electrical organs composed of muscle tissue lie on either side of the body disc and are filled with cells much like electrical plates in a battery. The shock of electric rays found in California is not strong enough to seriously injure a diver, but the discharge is powerful enough to get your attention and make you wish you had turned the other way.

## Great White Sharks

Great white sharks (*Carcharodon carcharius*) are found along the Central California coast, although their numbers are not as plentiful as the media would have you believe. They are predators and are drawn to areas where they can readily find an abundant food source. The Farallon Islands, 27 miles (43km) offshore of San Francisco, are known to be a favorite feeding ground for these sharks, primarily because harbor seals, California and Stellar sea lions, and elephant seals live and breed there. Año Nuevo State Park, south of Half Moon Bay, is the site of a large elephant seal rookery and the Marin Headlands also offers large numbers of pinnipeds. These three areas form what is known as the "red triangle," where great whites are commonly found. If divers want to avoid great whites they should stay out of this area. On rare occasions white sharks do make appearances in Monterey and on the north coast, but their portrayal as a menace is farfetched at best.

## Kelp

Kelp, though not inherently dangerous, presents two main problems for divers. First, it is easy to become entangled in kelp, especially at the surface, if you are not careful. When diving in a kelp bed, divers should take their time and be aware of their surroundings at all times. Always look up to find an opening in the kelp canopy before surfacing. If you do become entangled, never panic or thrash around. Just wait for your buddy to remove the problem kelp strands. It is easy to snap kelp stalks by doubling them over on themselves. The other danger kelp presents is simply from falling on slippery rock surfaces that are covered with kelp or algae.

# Diving
# Conservation
# & Awareness

Commercial fishing and kelp harvesting, recreational diving, industrial development, tourism and other human activities have placed incredible pressures on the marine environment along the California coast. Other commercial activities such as oil drilling and shipping also pose a serious threat to the survival of many types of marine life up and down the coast. Controversy rages as to who is at fault for serious reductions in the number and size of all species of rockfish and other bottom fish in general (e.g., cabezon and lingcod) along the central and north coast areas. Still more heated are the debates about what can and should be done to preserve existing resources and perhaps make it possible for endangered species to stage a comeback. A brief discussion of a few topics of ongoing debate follows.

## Rockfish Survival Threatened

Though rockfish were once seen in schools of thousands, divers today are fortunate to observe blue rockfish in schools of 50 to 100, and blacks are on the endangered species list. There is an ongoing debate as to why the numbers of rockfish have declined. Most species of rockfish are popular for commercial fishing, sport fishing and spearfishing. A major initial cause of rockfish depletion was commercial over-fishing by gill nets and long-line fishing, which are now restricted to deeper waters in an attempt to protect the remaining coastal fish populations. Unfortunately, now that rockfish populations are dangerously low, a significant take by any group would probably have a profound impact. In fact, all forms of fish taking, as well as pollution, sewage spills and coastal development now contribute to the problem.

## Live-Fish Fishing

Another form of commercial fishery has escaped regulation altogether: live-fish fishing, which prospers unrestricted in Southern California and now in the Monterey area. Baited traps resembling squat crab pots, and "tree fishing" devices made from PVC pipe are the most common means of live fishing. The industry targets smaller "plate-sized" fish, which are often not yet reproductive. Fish are taken live and sold primarily to California restaurants, but reportedly have been shipped to Asia as well. These fish are in such great demand that it is apparently economically feasible to ship them overseas in oxygenated containers, in a manner similar to aquarium fish transport. Unregulated live-fish fishing threatens to completely eliminate certain species from the entire region. Environmentalists hope that live-fish fishing will be suspended pending an environmental impact report.

## Declining Abalone Populations

In 1997, the Abalone Bill was signed by Governor Pete Wilson, prohibiting the recreational and commercial harvesting of all species of abalone from any state waters south of San Francisco. This moratorium will remain in effect for an indefinite period of time. The Department of Fish and Game is currently working on an abalone recovery and management plan. Commercial harvesting of abalone north of San Francisco currently remains closed.

The moratorium was put into effect as a result of a noted decline in Southern and Central California abalone populations, attributed to commercial and recreational overharvesting and a bacterial infection called abalone withering syndrome. Although abalone are still plentiful along the coastline of Sonoma and Mendocino Counties, additional restrictions are a possibility. Divers should always check with local dive stores for current regulations.

## Offshore Oil Wells & Shipping

Throughout the years, California has had to balance the economic benefits of offshore petroleum development and shipping against the adverse impacts to fisheries and marine resources. Concerns about the cumulative impact of these activities, along with a number of major marine oil spills in recent years, led to a complete moratorium on offshore oil and gas leasing in California state waters until 2008. However, the danger of oil leaks from tankers passing near shore still presents a potential hazard. The National Oceanic and Atmospheric Organization (NOAA) and the U.S. Coast Guard have made recommendations to Congress to regulate how and where vessels must travel as they move along the coast.

# Marine Reserves & Regulations

The State of California has jurisdiction over the marine environment, fish taking and kelp harvesting up to 3 miles (5km) offshore. The California Fish and Game Commission establishes regulations and the Department of Fish and Game enforces them. The only major exception with respect to these regulatory powers lies in the area of offshore fisheries and migratory species, which are regulated by the Pacific Fishery Management Council. Anyone who fishes (whether spearfishing, pole fishing or free-diving for abalone) is expected to know and follow current regulations and carry proper licenses.

Specific areas are designated as sanctuaries, refuges, reserves or preserves. Special regulations and protections apply in the following areas.

## Monterey Bay National Marine Sanctuary

In 1972 a federal law was passed allowing Congress to designate marine areas as sanctuaries. There are now 12 sanctuaries around the country. The Monterey Bay National Marine Sanctuary was designated in 1992. This area stretches 350 miles (560km) along the California coastline from the Marin headlands north of San

Francisco south to Cambria in San Luis Obispo County. The sanctuary extends from the high tide mark to as far as 53 miles (85km) offshore. It is the largest marine sanctuary in the United States and the second largest in the world (after the Great Barrier Reef in Australia).

While the sanctuary itself does not regulate or preclude sport, recreational or commercial fishing, it does prohibit divers from removing shipwreck artifacts or harassing marine mammals and places restrictions on jade collection within Jade Cove on the Big Sur coast. The sanctuary also has jurisdiction to prohibit mining on the sea floor and to preclude oil and gas exploration and development, as well as dumping. There are some shipping lanes through the sanctuary that pose dangers of oil spills to the marine environment.

## Hopkins Marine Life Refuge

The protected area extends from the mean high tide mark to a depth of 60ft (18m), from Third Street in Pacific Grove south to the Pacific Grove/Monterey border. Diving is allowed, but taking marine plants, fish and invertebrates is prohibited. Hopkins Marine Station conducts experiments within the borders of the refuge.

## Pacific Grove Marine Gardens Fish Refuge

This protected area extends south from Third Street in Pacific Grove (the edge of the Hopkins Marine Life Refuge) around Point Pinos to the Pacific Grove city

### Fish & Game Regulations and Licensing

The Department of Fish and Game was established to manage California's diverse fish, wildlife and plant resources, and the habitats upon which they depend, for their ecological values and for their use and enjoyment by the public. You can help preserve marine resources by purchasing appropriate fishing licenses and by following fishing regulations. Fishing licenses are available at convenience stores along the coast.

A variety of regulations and limits are placed on ocean fish and game collection. These may include limits on:

Species (some may not be taken)

Size (there is often a minimum)

Quantity (there is often a maximum)

Sex (some reproductive females may not be taken at specific times of year)

Region (some areas are protected or off-limits)

Time (time of day or night and of year)

Methods and Gear

For general information about licensing or regulations, contact the Department of Fish and Game (☎ 916-653-7664) or visit their website at www.dfg.ca.gov/dfghome.html. Specific information about regulations is outlined in the booklet "California Sport Fishing Regulations," available at no charge through many sporting goods stores throughout the state, and online at www.dfg.ca.gov/fg_comm/fishregs.pdf.

limits, including Asilomar State Beach. Boating and diving are allowed within the park. Fishing and spearfishing is permitted for finfish and eels. Taking any other marine life or shellfish is prohibited.

## Carmel Bay Ecological Reserve

The reserve includes all of Carmel Bay inside a line drawn from Pescadero Point (north of Carmel Bay) to Granite Point (south, near Point Lobos State Reserve). Fishing and spearfishing is permitted for finfish and eels. Taking any other marine life, shellfish or marine plants is prohibited.

## Point Lobos State Reserve

Reserve boundaries are approximately 500 yards (460m) from the shoreline. The northern boundary of the underwater portion of the reserve is a line drawn north-northwest from the western side of Granite Point. The southern reserve boundary is the line drawn due west from the stone house directly south of the mouth of Gibson Creek. Entry into the underwater park area is allowed only through the main gate of the park. Diving in Point Lobos is allowed only in the Whalers Cove and Bluefish Cove, by permit only. Fishing, spearfishing, and taking or disturbing any marine life within the reserve are prohibited.

Whaler's Cove is the only entry to this underwater park.

## California Coastal National Monument

In 2000, the California Coastal National Monument was established to protect all the exposed reefs, rocks and islands above the high-water mark that are owned by the U.S. government along the state's 840-mile coastline, within 12 miles of shore. These land formations are part of the near-shore ocean zone that begins just offshore and ends at the boundary between the continental shelf and the continental slope. The coastal monument is a biological treasure that provides habitat for sea lions, elephant seals and harbor seals. An estimated 200,000 breeding seabirds, including the endangered brown pelican, feed, perch and nest within the monument's boundaries.

# Responsible Diving

Dive sites tend to be located where the reefs and walls display the most beautiful marine life. By following certain basic guidelines while diving, you can help preserve the ecology and beauty of the reefs:

1. Practice and maintain proper buoyancy control and avoid over-weighting. Be aware that buoyancy can change over the period of an extended trip. Initially you may breathe harder and need more weighting; a few days later you may breathe more easily and need less weight. Tip: Use your weight belt and tank position to maintain a horizontal position—raise them to elevate your feet, lower them to elevate your upper body. Also be careful about buoyancy loss: As you go deeper, your wetsuit compresses, as does the air in your BC.

2. Avoid touching living marine organisms with your body and equipment. Though holding on to the mostly granite substrate normally doesn't do much damage, choose handholds carefully to avoid harming marine life.

3. Take great care in underwater caves, ledges and other tight areas. The heavy surge can be dangerous, throwing you into the rocks and walls. Divers should take turns inspecting these areas to lessen the danger.

4. Secure gauges, computer consoles and the octopus regulator so they're not dangling—they are like miniature wrecking balls to a reef and can become entangled in the kelp.

5. When swimming in strong currents, be extra careful about leg kicks and handholds.

6. Photographers should take extra precautions as cameras and equipment affect buoyancy. Changing f-stops, framing a subject and maintaining position for a photo often conspire to prohibit the ideal "no-touch" approach. When you must use "holdfasts," choose them intelligently.

7. Resist the temptation to collect or buy marine life souvenirs. Aside from the ecological damage, taking home marine souvenirs depletes the beauty of a site and spoils other divers' enjoyment.

8. Ensure that you take home all your trash. Plastics in particular pose a serious threat to marine life.

9. Resist the temptation to feed fish. You may disturb their normal eating habits, encourage aggressive behavior or feed them food that is detrimental to their health.

10. Minimize your disturbance of marine animals. There are regulations against making contact with or approaching sea otters, whales, seals and sea lions, as this can cause them great anxiety.

# Telephone Calls

If you are calling within the U.S., dial 1 + the area code and local 7-digit number. Toll-free (800 or 888) numbers can be accessed from the U.S. and, usually, Canada: dial 1 + the area code (800 or 888) + the 7-digit toll-free number.

# Accommodations

Northern California has a wide range of accommodations suitable for divers, ranging from basic to luxurious. The following resources supply information on motels, hotels, resorts, bed-and-breakfast inns and vacation rentals.

## Monterey Peninsula (Monterey & Carmel)

**Monterey Peninsula Visitors and Convention Bureau**
380 Alvarado St.
Monterey, CA 93940
☎ 831-649-1770
www.monterey.com

**Monterey County Travel and Tourism Alliance**
(online destination guide)
www.gomonterey.com

**Monterey Peninsula Reservations**
☎ 831-655-3487
Toll-free ☎ 888-655-3424
www.monterey-reservations.com

**Monterey Lodging**
P.O. Box 222197
Carmel, CA 93922
☎ 831-646-9686
www.montereylodging.com

**Time to Coast**
(fax-back accommodations listings)
Toll-free ☎ 800-555-9283

**Monterey Peninsula Chamber of Commerce**
380 Alvarado St.
Monterey, CA 93940
☎ 831-648-5360
www.mpcc.com

## Big Sur

**Big Sur Chamber of Commerce**
P.O. Box 87
Big Sur, CA 93920
☎ 831-667-2100
www.bigsurcalifornia.org

**John Rabold's Visitor's Guide to Big Sur**
www.jrabold.net/bigsur

## Sonoma

**Redwood Coast Chamber of Commerce**
P.O. Box 338
Gualala, CA 95445
Toll-free ☎ 800-778-5252
www.redwoodcoastchamber.com

**Rams Head Realty & Rentals**
(home rentals at Sea Ranch)
Toll-free ☎ 800-785-3455
fax: 707-785-2429
www.ramshead-realty.com

## Sonoma (continued)

**Sea Ranch Escape**
(home rentals at Sea Ranch)
☎ 707-785-2426
Toll-free ☎ 888-732-7262
fax: 707-785-2124
www.888searanch.com

**Sonoma County Tourism Information**
☎ 707-524-7589 (general)
Toll-free ☎ 800-510-2888 (lodging)

**Sea Ranch Rentals**
(home rentals at Sea Ranch)
P.O. Box 246
39200 Highway 1 South
Gualala, CA 95445
☎ 707-884-4235
www.searanchrentals.com

## Mendocino

**Fort Bragg-Mendocino Coast Chamber of Commerce**
P.O. Box 1141
or 332 North N. Main St.
Fort Bragg, CA 95437
☎ 707-961-6300
Toll-free ☎ 800-726-2780
www.mendocinocoast.com

**Mendocino Coast Reservations**
P.O. Box 1143
or 1000 Main St.
Mendocino, CA 95460
☎ 707-937-5033
Toll-free ☎ 800-262-7801
www.mendocinovacations.com

# State Parks

**California State Parks**
Toll-free ☎ 800-444-7275 (reservations within the U.S.)
☎ 916-638-5883 (international reservations)
www.cal-parks.ca.gov

**Point Lobos State Reserve**
Route 1, Box 62
Coast Highway 1
Carmel, CA 93923
☎ 831-624-8413 (diving reservations)
http://pt-lobos.parks.state.ca.us
ptlobos@mbay.net (email reservations)

**Salt Point State Park**
25050 Coast Highway 1
Jenner, CA 95450
☎ 707-847-3221 (general information and reservations)
☎ 707-847-3222 (recorded weather and tide information)
www.calparks.ca.gov/DISTRICTS/russian/spsp248.htm

**Fort Ross State Historic Park**
19005 Coast Highway 1
Jenner, CA 95450
☎ 707-847-3286
www.cal-parks.ca.gov/DISTRICTS/russian/frshp207.htm

**Russian Gulch State Park**
Coast Highway 1
Mendocino, CA 95460
☎ 707-937-5804 (Cal State Parks automated number, including reservations)
www.cal-parks.ca.gov/DISTRICTS/russian/mendo/rgsp141.htm

**Van Damme State Park**
Coast Highway 1
Little River, CA 95456
☎ 707-937-5804 (automated number, including reservations)
www.cal-parks.ca.gov/DISTRICTS/russian/mendo/vdsp142.htm

**Caspar Headlands State Reserve**
Coast Highway 1
Casper, CA 95420
☎ 707-937-5804 (automated number, including reservations)
www.cal-parks.ca.gov/DISTRICTS/russian/mendo/chsr160.htm

**MacKerricker Beach State Park**
Coast Highway 1
Fort Bragg, CA 95437
Toll-free ☎ 800-444-7275

# Private Campgrounds

## Sonoma County

**Ocean Cove Campground**
23125 Highway 1
Jenner, CA 95450
☎ 707-847-3422 (camping and airfill reservations)
☎ 707-847-3222 (recorded weather and tide information)

**Timber Cove Campground**
21350 Highway 1
Jenner, CA 95450
☎ 707-847-3278

## Mendocino County

**Albion River Flat Campground**
3540 North Highway 1
Albion, CA 95410
☎ 707-937-0606

**Schooner's Landing Campground**
33621 Albion River
Albion, CA 95410
☎ 707-937-5707

**Anchor Bay Campground**
P.O. Box 1529
or 35400 South Highway 1
Gualala, CA 95445
☎ 707-884-4222
www.abcamp.com

**Caspar Beach**
14441 Point Cabrillo Dr.
Mendocino, CA 95460
☎ 707-964-3306
www.gocampingamerica.com
/casparbeach/index

# Diving Services

The following dive shops offer a range of rental and retail gear and air fills. Many offer certification and advanced diving classes. All facilities should display their appropriate affiliations (NAUI, PADI, SSI, etc.). Most major credit cards are accepted.

## Monterey Area

**Aquarius Dive Shop**
2040 Del Monte Ave.
Monterey, CA 93940
☎ 831-375-1933

**Manta Ray Dive Center**
245 Foam St.
Monterey, CA 93940
☎ 831-375-6268
www.mantaraydive.com

**Aquarius II Dive Shop**
32 Cannery Row
Monterey, CA 93940
☎ 831-375-6605

**Monterey Bay Dive Center**
225 Cannery Row
Monterey, CA 93940
☎ 831-656-0454
Toll-free ☎ 800-607-2822
www.mbdc.to

**Bamboo Reef**
614 Lighthouse Ave.
Monterey, CA 93940
☎ 831-372-1685
www.citysearch.com/sfo/bambooreef

# Big Sur Area

**Depth Perceptions**
3280 N. Main
Los Osos, CA 93442
☎ 805-528-3631

**Dive Shop of Santa Maria**
1975 B Broadway
Santa Maria, CA 93454
☎ 805-922-0076

**Dive West Sports**
115 W. Main St.
Santa Maria, CA 94354
☎ 805-925-5878

# Santa Cruz Area

**Adventure Sports Unlimited**
303 Potrero Court, #15
Santa Cruz, CA 95060
☎ 831-458-3648
www.asudoit.com

**Aqua Safari Scuba Center**
231 Evergreen St.
Santa Cruz, CA 95060
☎ 831-476-2782

**Ocean Odyssey**
860 17th Ave.
Santa Cruz, CA 95062
☎ 831-475-3483
www.oceanodyssey.com

# San Jose/Peninsula Area

**Any Water Sports**
1344 Saratoga Ave.
San Jose, CA 95129
☎ 408-244-4433
Toll-free ☎ 800-408-3483
www.anywater.com

**Blue Water Divers**
1954A Old Middlefield Way
Mountain View, CA 94043
☎ 650-968-5992
Toll-free ☎ 800-746-3483
www.bwdiver.com

**Burlingame Dive Center & Scuba School**
390 Lang Rd.
Burlingame, CA 94010
☎ 650-579-1954

**Diver Dan's Wet Pleasure**
2245 El Camino Real
Santa Clara, CA 95050
☎ 408-984-5819
Toll-free ☎ 800-247-2822
www.diverdans.com

**Pacific Offshore Divers**
1188 Branham Lane
San Jose, CA 95118
☎ 408-265-3483
Toll-free ☎ 800-375-3483
www.podih2o.com

**Peninsula Diving Center**
1015 W. El Camino Real
Mountain View, CA 94040
☎ 650-965-2241
www.pendive.com

**Splash Aquatics**
2215 El Camino Real
Santa Clara, CA 95050
☎ 408-261-3483
www.splash-aquatics.com

**Stan's Skin and Scuba Diving**
554 S. Bascom Ave.
San Jose, CA 95128
☎ 408-998-0767

**Wallin's Dive Center**
1119 Industrial Rd.
San Carlos, CA 94070
☎ 650-591-5641
www.wallins.com

## San Francisco/East Bay Area

**Anchor Shack Skin Diving Center**
5775 Pacheco Blvd.
Pacheco, CA 94553
☎ 925-825-4960

**Anderson's Scuba Diving**
541 Oceana Blvd.
Pacifica, CA 94044
☎ 415-355-3050

**Bamboo Reef**
584 4th St.
San Francisco, CA 94107
☎ 415-362-6694
www.citysearch.com/sfo/bambooreef

**Cal Dive and Travel**
1750 6th St.
Berkeley, CA 94710
☎ 510-524-3248

**Captain Aqua's Dive Center**
40849 Fremont Blvd.
Fremont, CA 94538
☎ 510-490-5597

6715 Dublin Blvd.
Dublin, CA 94568
☎ 925-829-3283
www.captainaqua.com

**Dive N Board**
1776 Arnold Industrial Way, Suite O
Concord, CA 94520
☎ 925-689-6969

**Dive N Board**
990 Moraga Rd.
Lafayette, CA 94549
☎ 925-283-5400

**Nautilus Aquatics**
3264 Buskirk Ave.
Pleasant Hill, CA 94523
☎ 925-932-3483

**Nautilus Aquatics**
3140 Crow Canyon Rd.
San Ramon, CA 94583
☎ 925-275-9005

**Neon Reef Dive Shop**
22542 Second St.
Hayward, CA 94541
☎ 510-537-9715

**Ocean Quest Dive Center**
45301 Industrial Place, #2
Fremont, CA 94538
☎ 510-651-6000

**Original Steele's**
5987 Telegraph Ave.
Oakland, CA 94609
☎ 510-655-4344

**Undersea Adventures**
2550-G San Ramon Valley Blvd.
San Ramon, CA 94583
☎ 925-838-2348

## North Bay/North Coast Area

**Adventures Unlimited**
2086 Kirkland
Napa, CA 94559
☎ 707-255-3483

**Bodega Bay Pro Dive**
1275 Coast Highway 1
Bodega Bay, CA 94923
☎ 707-875-3054

**Dive Crazy Dive Shop**
33621 North Side Albion River Rd.
Albion, CA 95410
☎ 707-937-3079
www.divecrazy.com

**Harbor Dive Center**
200 Harbor Dr.
Sausalito, CA 94965
☎ 415-331-0904

**Marin Skin Diving**
3765 Redwood Highway
San Rafael, CA 94903
☎ 415-479-4332

**Napa Dive and Sport**
162 S. Coombs St.
Napa, CA 94559
☎ 707-257-2822

**North Coast Discoveries (Tours)**
P.O. Box 951
Mendocino, CA 95460
☎ 707-961-1566

**North Coast Scuba**
J. Baker True Value Hardware
38820 Coast Highway 1
Gualala, CA 95445
☎ 707-884-3534

# North Bay/North Coast Area (continued)

**Petaluma Sport Shop and Dive**
884 Bodega Ave.
Petaluma, CA 94952
☎ 415-763-0930

**Pinnacles Dive Center**
2112 Armory Drive
Santa Rosa, CA 95401
☎ 707-542-3100
Toll-free ☎ 800-439-3483

**Pro Sport Center**
508 Myrtle Ave.
Eureka, CA 95501
☎ 707-443-6328

**Rohnert Park Dive & Travel**
5665 Redwood Dr., Suite B
Rohnert Park, CA 94928
☎ 707-584-2323
www.rpdc.com

**Sonoma Coast Bamboo Reef**
5702 Commerce Blvd.
Rohnert Park, CA 94928
☎ 707-586-0272
www.sc-bambooreef.com

**Sub Surface Progression**
18600 North Highway 1
Fort Bragg, CA 95437
☎ 707-964-3793

# Sacramento/Central Valley Area

**Aqua Divers**
300 Carriage Square
Yuba City, CA 95991
☎ 916-671-3483

**Aqua Sports**
1616 E. Shields Ave.
Fresno, CA 93704
☎ 559-224-0744

**Aquatic Dreams Scuba Center**
1212 Kansas Ave.
Modesto, CA 95351
☎ 209-577-3483

**Bob's Dive Shop**
4374 N. Blackstone
Fresno, CA 92726
☎ 559-225-3483

**Dolphin Scuba Center**
1530 El Camino Ave.
Sacramento, CA 95821
☎ 916-929-8188

**Elk Grove Diving Center**
9257 Elk Grove Blvd.
Elk Grove, CA 95624
☎ 916-686-1122

**High Sierra Divers**
217 Palm Ave.
Auburn, CA 95603
☎ 530-823-6757

**Hudson Family Dive Center**
4110 Datsun Court
Shingle Springs, CA 95682
☎ 530-676-9011

**Mother Lode Skin Diving Shop**
2020 H St.
Sacramento, CA 95814
☎ 916-446-4041

**Nautilus Diving & Sports Center**
4930 Pacific St.
Rocklin, CA 95677
☎ 916-624-3483

**Pacific Reef Scuba**
615 Merchant St., Suite B
Vacaville, CA 95688
☎ 707-448-3483
www.pacreef.com

**Scuba Plus**
3255 Hammer Lane
Stockton, CA 95209
☎ 209-957-2822

**Scuba World Sacramento**
5112 Madison Ave.
Sacramento, CA 95841
☎ 916-332-8294

**Sports Cove**
1410 E. Monte Vista
Vacaville, CA 95688
☎ 707-448-9454

**Stockton Aquatic Center**
1127 W. Fremont St
Stockton, CA 95203
☎ 209-467-3483

# Dive Boat Operations

**Marin Skin Diving**
3765 Redwood Highway
San Rafael, CA 94903
☎ 415-479-4332
*Beach Hopper II*
30-ft boat, 12 divers
Home port: Monterey
Destinations: Monterey Bay, Carmel Bay

**Cypress Charters**
1344 Saratoga Ave.
San Jose, CA 95129
☎ 408-244-4433
www.cypresscharters.com
webmaster@anywater.com
*Cypress Sea*
50-ft boat, 20 divers
*Cypress Point*
60-ft boat, 20 divers
Home port: Monterey
Destinations: Monterey Bay, Carmel Bay

**Monterey Express**
3 Paso Del Rio
Carmel, CA
☎ 831-659-3009
Toll-free ☎ 888-422-2999
www.montereyexpress.com
capttim@montereyexpress.com
*Monterey Express*
42-ft boat, 20 divers
Home Port: Monterey
Destinations: Monterey Bay, Carmel Bay

**Monterey Scuba Charters**
761 Lighthouse Ave.
Monterey, CA 93940
☎ 831-375-2200
fax: 831-375-1636
www.divemonterey.com
msc@divemonterey.com
*Beach Hopper II*
30-ft boat, 12 divers/tourists
Home port: Monterey
Destinations: Monterey Bay, Carmel Bay

**Monterey Bay Dive Center**
225 Cannery Row
Monterey, CA 93940
☎ 831-656-0454
Toll-free ☎ 800-607-2822
www.mbdc.to
service@mbdc.to
*Silver Prince*
40-ft boat, 14 divers
Home Port: Monterey
Destinations: Monterey Bay, Carmel Bay

**Dive Crazy**
P.O. Box 130
Albion, CA 95410
☎ 707-937-3079
*Dive Crazy*
27-ft boat, 6 divers
www.divecrazy.com
divecrazy@humboldt.net
Home Port: Albion
Destinations: Mendocino Coast

# Underwater Photography & Video

**Backscatter**
(Underwater photography and video)
32 Cannery Row
Monterey, CA 93940
☎ 831-645-1082
www.backscatter.com

**Camera Tech**
(Photography and video equipment)
1801 Balboa
San Francisco, CA
☎ 415-387-1700

**Light & Motion**
(Video)
300 Cannery Row
Monterey, CA 93940
☎ 831-645-1525

# Marine Conservation Organizations

**California Artificial Reef
Enhancement Program**
Toll-free ☎ 800-804-6002
www.calreefs.org

**Coalition for Enhanced Marine Resources**
Toll-free ☎ 800-604-5007
www.preservereefs.org

**Save Our Shores**
☎ 831-462-5660
www.saveourshores.org

**Surfrider Foundation USA**
☎ 949-492-8170
www.surfrider.org

# Other Resources

**Air One**
Mobile Airfills (Monterey)
☎ 408-655-1611

**ba_diving**
(electronic mailing list for Northern
California divers)
www.best.com/~kylem
ba_diving-request@lists.best.com

**California Department of Fish & Game**
www.dfg.ca.gov/dfghome.html

**Central California Diving Council**
(coalition of Northern and Central California
dive clubs)
P.O. Box 779
Daly City, CA 94017
☎ 415-583-8492
www.cencal.org

**Monterey County Health Department
Beach Hotline**
(info on beach closures due to elevated
bacteria levels)
Toll-free ☎ 800-347-6363

**Monterey Peninsula Underwater
Photographers**
http://home.netcom.com/~mpup

**National Weather Service Marine
Weather Page**
www.nws.mbay.net/marine.html

**National Weather Service Tide Tables**
www.nws.mbay.net/sunset.html#mry_tide

**Northern California Underwater
Photographic Society**
www.ncups.org

# Useful General Websites

**Chuck Tribolet's site**
www.garlic.com/~triblet/swell/

**Rocky Daniel's site**
www.sonic.net/~rocky/index.htm

**Scuba California**
www.scubacalifornia.com

**Tim Ewing's site**
http://pw1.netcom.com/~time2div
/scubamain.html

# Index

dive sites covered in this book appear in **bold** type